MORE
MOUNTAIN
SPIRITS

MORE MOUNTAIN SPIRITS

THE CONTINUING CHRONICLE OF
Moonshine Life
and
Corn Whiskey, Wines, Ciders & Beers
in
America's Appalachians

JOSEPH EARL DABNEY

Bright Mountain Books, Inc.
Fairview, North Carolina

Printed in the United States of America

ISBN: 0-914875-03-5
EAN: 978-0914875-03-1
(Previously published by Copple House Books as *Mountain Spirits II*, ISBN: 0-932298-05-2)

Library of Congress Cataloging in Publication Data

Dabney, Joseph Earl.
    More mountain spirits.
    Reprint. Originally published: Mountain spirits II.
Lakemont, Ga : Copple House Books, c1980.
    1. Whiskey —Southern States —History. 2. Alcoholic beverages —Southern States —History. 3. Distilling, Illicit — Southern States —History. I. Title.
TP605.D24 1985   663'.5'00975   85-10932
ISBN: 0-914875-03-5

Dedicated to the memory of
Simmie Free, free spirit of
the mountains

CONTENTS

Foreword

After the publication of my first book on The Decline and Fall of Corn Whiskey as a Fine Art—otherwise known as *MOUNTAIN SPIRITS* and sometimes by its sub-title, *A Chronicle of Corn Whiskey from King James' Ulster Plantation to America's Appalachians*—I ran into scores of people who had even greater tales to tell me about this fading era of Americana. Their grandpoppas and poppas and uncles had experiences that would fill another book, they said, giving truth to the saying that you couldn't walk a mile along almost any "branch" in the Southeastern hill country without coming across the ruins of a 'still.

It appeared to me that perhaps it would be worthwhile to retrace some of my steps through the north Georgia Appalachians to ferret out these stories and so I did just that. The project proved to be a delightful excursion and I got to meet a number of additional personalities who shared with me their experiences. Such Georgia mountain people as Theodore King of Hiawassee, Maud Thacker of Tate, Verner Fox of Dial, Stanley Reed of Ellijay and Taft Densmore of Amicalola Falls.

When you add these to the scores of characters I had interviewed in researching *MOUNTAIN SPIRITS*, and re-met on this tour, such as Simmie Free of Tiger, Hubert Howell of Cartersville, Buck Carver of Dillard, John Henry Chumley of Dawsonville, Fred Goswick of Marietta and Hamper McBee of Monteagle, Tennessee, plux ex-revenooers Duff Floyd of Jasper, James Stratigos of Gainesville, Jesse James Bailey of Asheville, North Carolina, Frank Rickman of Clayton, David Ayers of Cornelia and Homer Powell of Marietta, it became apparent once again that the spirits story was not an isolated or parochial one, but the saga of a sub-culture extending throughout an entire region.

First grain whiskey made in America, according to some sources, was distilled at Berkeley Plantation, Virginia, in 1621 and 1622. The beverage, wrote Captain George Thorpe, its maker, was "a brew of corn and maize . . . much better than British Ale." Thorpe unfortunately was killed in 1622 by drunken Indians before he was able to perfect his American drink. This painting illustrates the type of crude distillery probably in operation.

On this tour, I learned of the broader picture of mountain spirits of days past—such mountain beverages as brandies, beers, wines and ciders, along with more details about corn whiskey.

So I am delighted to be able to share with readers the results of this latest foray into the foothills, parts of which were published in a small volume in the interim.

The decline and fall of home-made mountain spirits is confirmed by no less an authority than the bumptious "Hee Haw" personality Junior Samples. But on occasion even he turns nostalgic when looking back on the days when he took turns saw-milling and making moonshine around Coal Mountain! "We always knew we would get caught. But in the dead of winter, when the flour barrel got low, we made us a little whiskey . . . ."

For Atlanta, there has been a strong affinity with mountain spirits, inasmuch as this city was not only the primary market for the hill-country booze, but the magnet for the good ole boys who hauled in the whiskey during the week and raced at Lakewood's dirt speedway on Sundays.

Many Atlantans will never forget the days when the trippers, driving their black Ford coupes, whipped out of the hills into the then suburb of Buckhead, smashing police barricades, darting into side streets, getting their contraband through to their bootlegger customers in the city.

One of Atlanta's real characters of that pre-World War II period was "Blind Willie," a black troubadour who strolled around the parking lot of the Blue Lantern on Ponce de Leon Avenue, twanging on his 12-string guitar for tips and drinks. His favorite expression, regardless of the size bottle given him, was, "Jest throw away the cap."

Georgia Tech students loved to drive into the Blue Lantern to quaff draft beer and listen to Blind Willie's wild and ribald original compositions. A student remembered Blind Willie as being no candidate for beauty. "You could have raked the ugly off him with a stick," he recalled, and his voice was something between an organ-grinder's music and an unoiled door hinge, channeled around a cud of tobacco in his jaw.

The story was that Blind Willie went blind drinking bad whiskey during prohibition. In any event, he gave soul to that big guitar, plunking out blues, mostly. One of his original compositions was dedicated to a well-known liquor tripper of that period:

He's trouble in a Cadillac
He's a mess in a Ford V-8
I got to repeat, he don't never retreat
He's the runningist guy to hit this state

If you want some hot toddy
Give him a ring and a call
Don't get funny, wait and save your money
All the women screamin' Roy Hall

Blind Willie McTell

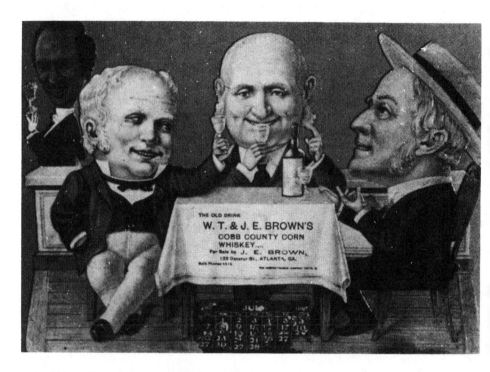

This old calendar from 1907 is an advertisement for Brown's "Cobb County Corn Whiskey," sold by the firm of J.E. Brown in Atlanta and made in adjacent Cobb County. The calendar itself was almost incidental. It is the small tablet underneath the table. This piece of art, in color, featured the heads in bas relief. That's the bartender in background. Georgia "went dry" in 1907 and whiskey making became illegal. National Prohibition began in 1919 and lasted until 1933.

This book does not go deeply into whiskey-tripping. Nor does it go into the historical perspective of whiskey-making in America and its roots in Scotland and Ireland. For these phases of the spirits saga, you might like to read my earlier book, *MOUNTAIN SPIRITS*.

One last word. Please read *MORE MOUNTAIN SPIRITS* in good spirits. But take warning. It is a federal offense for an individual to distill whiskey or brandy. Federal laws permit a homeowner (with a federal permit) to ferment at his home 200 gallons of wine or beer a year But distillation is a different matter and the violation

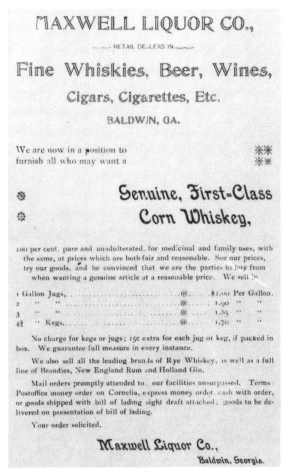

This advertisement from the late 1800s promotes "genuine, first-class corn whiskey" produced at the government licensed Maxwell distillery, Baldwin, Georgia. The whiskey was shipped over Georgia from Baldwin, being sold at prices of $1.70 to $2.00 per gallon, depending on the amount purchased. The distillery was located at "Stillhouse Hollow" next to Baldwin Mountain south of the little town of Baldwin, Georgia. The distillery was operated by the late J.L. Maxwell, whose son, the late L.F. Maxwell at one time operated a spirits place in Baldwin known as "The Barrel." It was built in the shape of a barrel and its advertisements read: "On a hot day come to the shady side of Baldwin to the barrel and get something for thy stomach's sake." Maxwell later closed "The Barrel" and operated a general merchandise store in Cornelia, Georgia.

of any one count of the federal liquor laws can subject one to a fine of up to $10,000 and/or ten years of imprisonment. This includes the making or selling of untaxpaid spirits.

Thus this book is one that you should read strictly for its humor content.

Joseph Earl Dabney

Atlanta, Ga.
Fall, 1980

Chapter
1

Simmie Free

"I usta raise dogs, cattle, hogs and make likker and brandy. That's a good combination . . . Ay God, I done a little of everything in the world, but I've always enjoyed everything I've done."

Simmie Free

Simmie Free was one of the colorful scions of the Appalachian country. Retired federal revenuer James Stratigos first told me about Simmie. If I wanted to learn about how mountain spirits were produced in the old days and in the old ways, Simmie, then in his 80's, would be worth a visit. I first visited Simmie in 1972, and went back many times since.

Rabun County is a storybook land . . . majestic mountains and rushing streams; glistening lakes and quiet, lush valleys. I found Simmie's farm not far from the Tallulah River, on a plateau overlooking a little creek and bottomlands.

As I drove up for the first time, unannounced and unintroduced, the old gentleman came out on his back porch and gave me a warm and hearthy handshake. He was wiry and ruddy-faced, standing about five feet four and wearing gallused overalls much too big for his small stature. Simmie was in fine humor and quickly invited me into his little frame home. He introduced me to his wife and asked her, "Do you know this young man?"

"Never seen him before in my life." she said.

"I ain't neither," Simmie replied. "But we're glad to have ye. Sit down."

An impish little man with an expressive face and bright, twinkling blue eyes, and an overwhelming sense of outrageous humor, Simmie Free turned out to be the most informative person I met in three years of touring the Appalachians during my spare time with my tape recorder.

On my first visit with Simmie, we went out on his front porch and looked at the ring of mountains.

"You've got a beautiful place here," I said.

"Yeah, here I am 82 and a half years old, jest got my home paid fer and now too old to see to it." He began to describe his place. "All that mountain away back thar's got five thousand dollars worth of timber on it. Hit belongs to me. Half the creek down yonder's mine. Goes up this way—up in yander. My land ain't never been measured. Don't know how many acres I got. I got six acres of bottomland here. As good a bottomland as there is in the world."

Looking over the rim of mountains all around the west, he said, "Take this'n right here. Right straight to the left. That's the Marcus Mountain. This little mountain here (the next one) they call that the Watts Mountain."

"Like Grandpa Watts?"

"It is Grandpa Watts and Watts and Watts and Watts on top of Watts. Watt's own all down this creek nearly to Tiger.

"And then, this mountain right here, you see that gap? That's Davis Gap. Then you see that *long* ledge of mountains yonder? Now you know the name of *that* mountain? That's Jabon Mountain."

"How do you spell that?" I asked.

"I'll be damned if I know," he replied. "We've fox hunted a lot, used to, on it and everything. And then the next little mountain yonder, right to the right of it, it is Tiger Mountain. Great big mountain.

"Yes sir, here's a purty, *purty* place to live. My land goes down to the creek and up to the top of the mountain to where the water divides it to the top of that ridge. What goes that way is hisn't (a neighbor), and what comes this way is mine. Half the creek's mine. Got rainbows in there and brown trout and horney heads and just all kinds of fish; bream too."

I asked Simmie to tell me about corn whiskey, as we sat together and rocked in his double-sized rocking chair.

"Here I am, eighty two and a half years old. *Still drinkin'* corn whiskey. The only thing that's kept me alive. Only thing. I'd been dead fifteen year, twenty year ago, hadn't been for that. It's better'n any medicine a doctor ever had. Now my wife there, she's never taken a drop of whiskey in her life. She don't believe it's good medicine."

"No I don't," Mrs. Annie said emphatically, stopping momentarily from rocking.

"Well, I do better when I got it than when I ain't got it," Simmie declared. "Hyar's my father," he said, pointing to a tintype portrait. "He's dead now. He was a hundred and nine year and four months old. And," he added with a wink, "the old devil just fooled around and let likker kill him! Me and the preacher told hit on him. Well, he did have good likker when he died 'cause I made it and carried it to him; he didn't die for the want of it."

"Well," I inquired, "tell me what it is that's so good about corn whiskey."

"I can't tell you, but I'm damned shore I know how it tastes and how to make it. I got the record of makin' the best they is in the state of Georgia, anywhar. I was born in Rabun County and moved up and lived in North Caroliny, South Caroliny and Tennessee. But here I made my home. Here's the first land I ever owned in my life. I come here and bought ever inch of it on credit. But I went to work and I went to makin' likker and sellin' likker—

Simmie Free loves children. The author's son Chris was with him on a visit and Simmie directed him to a big pear tree. "You like pears, don't you son? Well, they's a trail right up under that tree yonder. You can pick you up a bucketful 'fore you know it. Fill 'um plum full. Don't come back here with an empty bucket. That's what I tell *my* younguns."

"Now this place belongs to me and here I am . . . ." Simmie Free shows off patch of corn behind his home. At the time the photo was made, a man drove up looking for pears and said, "You've got a pretty place up here. Got any possums or coons up in there?" pointing to a wooded hillside. "Well," said Simmie, "I ain't gonna tell you what's up thar. You might be some kind of law and I've been aggravated with 'em and might be something up there that'd be dangerous."

a dollar a gallon. Now this place belongs to me and here I am, jest got my home paid for and now too old to see to it. Bought every penny of it on credit.

"When did I buy it? I don't know. Annie, you remember what year I bought this place?"

Mrs. Annie spoke up reluctantly, wary of talking to a stranger. "We came here in 1939 or 1938, I don't remember which. We moved down here the day after Christmas."

The old man said, "Me and her's lived together, how many years, Annie? Raised nine children. Two's dead and seven's living and they all married off, and got their own homes. They don't look to me and their mother for nothin'."

Then he returned to whiskey, his gravelly voice warming to his subject. Now crippled with arthirtis, Simmie was literally raised to love corn whiskey.

"My daddy said they went to given' corn whiskey to me when I was shore enough young, just a toddler, when they couldn't give me but one drop of sweetened likker. Then he said it wuddn't long until I got to where I could take two drops, then he said, it wuddn't but a day or two 'til I got to where I could take a half a teaspoonful. Then it wuddn't but a few days to where I could take a bottle and take a drink. I knew how to handle it. Didn't never get drunk. I could carry it all day. I'd go so fer and quit. Mother, she'd take a drink, but you couldn't say drinkin', you know. Her father and mother did. All the old people usta drink. Pa used to. We lived nineteen years in one house, rented house, and he always kept it in a ten-gallon kag, just settin' right in what they called the kitchen, out just as open as it could be. But all of his kids knowed not to tech it. You wouldn't take a drop *at-tall* out of it. If we drank any likker, we waited 'till he give it to us. He learnt us to leave it alone where he set it out. He wouldn't let us give it to our little friends and he wouldn't give it to minor children visitors. When kin folks would come in, he'd put a bottle or a jug on the table and pour 'em out a glass. Everybody kept a little flask of likker in his pocket. And you was allowed four gallons and three quarts on your wagon back then. But you wasn't allowed five."

"I learnt likker-making from my father. He and his daddy moved in here to these Georgia hills from up at Highlands, North Carolina. Granddaddy had a grist mill that made corn meal. He was an old Confederate soldier. I'm named for him. I don't know what our family was. More Irish than anything. Pa said I was and I guess he ought to know.

"Now, my boys don't drink. What about that. Me, I made it and drank it all my life and raised my boys and they don't drink! When the boys were young, I'd give likker to 'em anytime they wanted it. I learned 'em to do it right. Take it and then know when to quit. I *believe* in givin' it to a kid. I believe in lettin' him learn and know what it is, but I believed in learnin' him when to let it alone.

"My kids all know me. I could just look at one. I wouldn't have to tell him nothin' the second time, and I didn't whup 'em or nothin'. I wouldn't slap one's jaw; I wouldn't paddle one no way in the world. I just used a little keen hickory and one time would break 'em . . . yeah.

"Back when I got back married, in 1916, I was young and I didn't have nothin' to start off with. Got no money and nothin' to do with. Back then you couldn't get work to do. If you could get work with a man on a farm, you'd put in ten hours, even if it was down in a ditch, ditchin', ten hours for a dollar. Maybe twelve hours. Sunup to sundown. So when you got a dollar for a gallon of whiskey, that was big money. *Big* money. A lotta times, I've made a many and many a gallon and have to take ninety cents. Me and my daddy usta tote it through the woods from here to Clayton, about seven miles and a half. We'd tote it that fer. I'd tote a little three-gallon kag (twenty-four pounds, plus the keg) and he'd take a five-gallon kag. Go through the woods and tote it to a man and then get only a dollar a gallon. That was back in old Hoover's time. Old Hoover liked to perished everybody to death. Whiskey

Simmie Free, then 82, enjoyed himself at the First Annual Appalachian Ex-Moonshiners and Revenuers Convention at Gold Hills of Dahlonega. He was accompanied to the convention by Frank Rickman (L), his relative and son of the late and beloved sheriff of Rabun County for 24 years, Luther Rickman.

price went down to a dollar a gallon. It was down everywhere. I've sold many a half gallon for a quarter, just to get twenty-five cents. You know, they wasn't no money around. Only thing that saved us, we grew most of our vegetables and meat. You'd buy only sugar and coffee and that was somethin' you couldn't hardly get. You couldn't find it. Even flour, when you could get some, you could get only a pound or a pound and a half at a time. Had to eat cornbread three times a day. We'd mix it up with sorghum molasses. That was back in old Hoover's time."

At the time we talked Simmie was planning for the upcoming primary election. "I'm a gonna to go Tuesday to vote and I *always* drink on election. I always take my own. I went up there and drank with the sheriff on the last election day. He'll give me a drink just as quick as anybody in the country will. Him or his wife, either one. If he's not there, she will. Don't even have to ask her about it. She'll just go get a glass and pour it out and bring it to you." The first man he ever voted for when he was 21 years old was the late Eugene Talmadge, governor of Georgia, "and I've voted for a Talmadge ever since. Herman's a good feller. He come down here at Clayton at the new hotel. He stayed one night. I went up to Clayton. He'd done gone to bed, between ten and eleven o'clock. The clerk told me had already retired. I said, 'I don't care. I'd just as soon wake him up as anybody.' So he took me up to his room, and offered to set me up a bed in the room. No, I said, just want to stay with him about an hour. I went up there and woke him up. He got up and we spent an hour together . . . I don't know but I believe they'll come back to a Democratic president this time. I don't want to lose my vote but I'll try. I've never voted nothin' else but a straight Democratic ticket and I've voted a long time."

With a little bit of coaching, I got Simmie to give me some more of his recollections of whiskey-making, in the old days and in the old ways.

"I went to helpin' my daddy make likker when I wuddn't but nine year old. My daddy just let me go to the still with him and I watched him and learnt it myself. Same thing about farmin' and layin' off corn ground, takin' your hoe and hoeing corn. When I started, I didn't know they was any likker in sugar. I made it out of corn meal, rye and nothin' else.

"I lived up on the orchard on Glassy Mountain, set out every tree they is up there, and that's where all the pretty apples come from, lived up there seven years. Worked for ten cents an hour.

And sending my kids to school, tryin' to get 'em educated. My daddy couldn't read nor write, my mother couldn't read nor write. My oldest sister couldn't read nor write. I got as far as the second grade. Never did get any further. They always let me go a huntin' and not to school. That's where they made a mistake. But I got to where I could read and write pretty good. Up at the orchard, we worked thirty-five hands and I kept the time for all of 'um. But I sent my kids to school, tryin' to get 'em educated. Now all my boys got their homes and are doin' well. They don't fool with likker. They got good jobs.

"I'll tell you I've had a *hard time* all my life, but *I've always proved to be honest.* If you don't think I am, go up there and ask the banker in Clayton. Ask ever merchant they is in the county. They know me.

"Making likker, that's hard work. It's worsn't hard. I've picked up sugar where I usta have an old house on my place. I'd pick up a hundred pounds of sugar and go two miles and a half, way back across a mountain and put it on and make likker and then get a ten gallon kag full of likker (80 pounds), put it on my shoulder and tote it back home. Heck, I usta be stout as a mule. I could swing a ten-gallon kag on my shoulder and tote it from here to Clayton. Even if it was full. There's a way to do anything. If you step right and walk right, it'll stay up okay. I knew a feller who dropped a ten-gallon kag and it broke his leg, just as clean, in two.

"Yeah, makin' likker's hard work. I'd pick up two bushels of corn meal at that old house and go plum across the mountain, nearly two miles, carrying two bushels at a time on my shoulder. Weighed ninety-six pounds. We bought the meal from Talmadge's Grist Mill in Athens, three dollars a bushel, usta be, way back yonder, for corn meal. Ninety-six pounds to the sack. But I didn't care any more about that than nothin'. Pick it up and go on. If I was goin' up a long mountain, I'd just throw it down and set on it and rest, then pick it up and go on. Same with a ten-gallon kag. Back then, though, I could have toted one from here to Hollywood (Georgia), seven and a half miles and never set it down.

"Yeah, I drunk a lot of corn likker in my time. Now you can't hardly get it. People don't make pure corn. They don't make nothin' right no more. Now, good sugar likker's *good*, though. But all this old bastard beading stuff they make it out of, hell, it'd kill a dead snake . . . it'd kill a dead snake. Make it on old tin, sheet arn, anything, but what they ort to.

"I been caught and served four sentences in jail and then went

CONVENTION CELEBRANTS—Simmie Free (C) is pictured enjoying the First Annual Appalachian Ex-Moonshiners and Revenuers Convention in Dahlonega, Ga. with Frank Rickman (R) of Clayton, Ga., a relative, and author Joseph Dabney (L) of Atlanta.

on to the peniteniary 'fore I quit. I didn't care. I wanted to see the world anyhow. Went down there and stayed two months and fifteen days, come right back home, and if I didn't have a still, I'd have another made and have it in the furnace the next day.

"I bought my farm on credit for $480. Paid $80 down and borrowed the rest from the bank. Paid every penny of it sellin' likker. Ever inch of it. Used to, when I was bootleggin', the hill around my house would be covered with cars, people comin' to get likker. Sold it for a dollar a gallon. I'd sell a quart and give away a gallon!

"One time I got caught, I was comin' back from the mail box and the federal man wuz here. They had my still. Helt ten gallons. I knowed what to do—just go down there and plead guilty to it.

"We'd been down to get the mail and came back and the Revenue was up at home and said they had a report that I had a still up there. I said, 'Well, that's yourn's business. Just go ahead and do like you want to.' They went on up there and got it and brought it down to the house. Said they couldn't find the cap, the thump post and the headache piece. I had a second still, a brand new 'un, a little piece from the other'n, and I was afraid they'd get to lookin' for those pieces and find my other still. I decided to tell them right where to go. I said, 'Just go right up there to the mouth of the furnace, step across where the water comes down and that third trash pile and look under it and you'll find the rest of the outfit.' They went up there and got it and brought it down and cut it up and give it to me. I said, 'Well, I'll sell that copper for junk and buy me another half pint of whiskey.' And that's what I done with it. Went to court and pled guilty to it and come clear. I told the truth all the way through. You can't lie out of nothin'. I don't believe in it. I'd rather serve time as to tell a lie.

"Feller I'd sold some land to . . . he loved likker bettern' anything. Got to stealing likker from me all the time. I noticed I was gettin' cut up ever since I sold him that land and I'd have to go build time in jail, you know. Well, boys, I got enough of that. Then when the Revenue got that littlun above my pear tree— ten gallons, what it helt (I'd got the best still maker around, to make it for me, solid copper)—when they got that still, I'd had enough. This feller I sold this land to, he drank ever drop he could get and stole ever bit he could from me, then he *reported* me. Reported to the Federal law. The county law wouldn't have hurt me so bad, but the Federal law come and they cut it up. So I met him (the reporter) right down below the house in the road. I had no gun a-tall. He was a heap bigger than I was, but the hell it didn't make no difference to me. He drove up in his car. I said, 'STOP, here . . . *stop*! I want to know why the God damn hell you been doin' me like you have fer?' I'd been down to Gainesville and looked on the record book and found out what he'd been doin'. Reportin'. Yeah. Reported my boy and one of my nephews and him and his wife both signed that report and they got a hundred and forty-five dollars for reportin' my boy. I reached up and got him by the shoulder and I said, 'I just want you out here on this ground one minute.' I couldn't pull that sonofabitch out of that car to save my life and I'm pretty stout, and I was mad. He knowed I was mad. I gave him twenty-four hours to get out of there not not come back, or die. He left that night and he never did come back. He sent and got his things. Went and moved to Dahlonega and he got up there and done the same thing up there and they done the same thing that I done. Run him off. He stopped by the store and told some of 'um, 'You can tell Simmie

Free I'm a-goin' back down home to Gum Log. Never will come back to this country, anywhere.' He moved out before he sold it. A reporter is the low downdest white man that's ever drawed a breath. He ain't a white man if he is a reporter. I'd kill the damn fool. A reporter and a straight out damn thief. I like to set down a gallon of likker if I want to and leave it settin' out here, and if I got corn in the crib, I'd like for it to stay in there.

"No sir, I don't like a reporter. I don't like a rogue. I don't want 'em to steal what I got. If he wants anything, let him come and ask me and I'll give it to him if I want to and if I don't, I'll tell him he ain't gonna git it. Pa told me to always be shore and not bother nothin' that belonged to anybody else and as long as I didn't bother anybody else's stuff I wouldn't have any trouble.

"I usta raise dogs, cattle, hogs and make likker and brandy. That's a *good* combination. And I *always* had a big garden. Ay God, I done a little of everything in the world, but I've always enjoyed everything I've done. Right there on two terraces, I made 240 gallons of home made syrup. Outa cane. You could eat it with biscuits or with cornbread. I like it. That's the best eatin' there is. I like frash (sic) pork, backbone and ribs and I like to

"Simmie checks the proof" at Annual Appalachian Ex-Moonshiners & Revenuers Day, Dahlonega, Ga. L-R: Frank Rickman, Free, Joseph Dabney.

have syrup to eat 'em with. Frash, you know. I usta sell hogs. I've done everything that a man could do. But I always made good on anything I set my head to do. But back then, I sent my kids to school. Have nine kids and two of 'em died. But we got 'em through somehow."

As I started to leave, Simmie motioned me to keep my seat. "I enjoy ye bein' here. Lotta people in Rabun County comes to talk to us, we enjoy it. Ain't nothin' in the world I like better than my friends. I'd rather have friends than money. But if you ain't got no friends, you can't get nothin'. Money ain't so good if you don't have no friends. I'll tell you, you can spend your money, but if you've got a good honest friend, you won't spend him. I think more of my friends than anybody in the world and I got lots of them. If you don't believe it, just go up and see me in town. Everybody you'll hear 'em hollerin' at me from just ever direction. I got the name of bein' the worst man in the county to shake hands with people. God, I like to let 'em know I like 'em. Like to speak to 'em. I generally go about half lit anyhow. No matter. Polices, sheriff and all of 'um. Give a drink to the judge and all. But they like for theirs to be slipped around to 'um. They don't want it in the open. Used to, the one that sent me to the penny-tentiary, boy, he'd drink it with me. I'd take him a gallon at a time. I liked him because he'd drink with me. I'd carry him a gallon at a time . . . Set around and drink with me.

"I lived in Gainesville for eight months after I was married. I was servin' time down there (in the Hall County Jail). I had a room downstairs. Stayed thar eight months. Eight-one Maple Street there in Gainesville. That'uz the jail house. I could come (home on leave) to see my wife over at her father's and make some whiskey and take it back to Gainesville and sell it."

As I got up to leave, the old man said, "Don't go now; we'll go in and cut on the lights and rest some and then we'll set down at the table and have some supper."

I excused myself, however, and he walked with me out to the back porch to bid me good-bye. "You'ns come back. I *shore* have enjoyed talkin' to you."

Simmie stood and waved for a long time as I drove away on the winding road back to Tiger.

Simmie Free died on May 26, 1980, in a hospital near Clayton, Georgia. He was 88.

The author was privileged to visit Simmie in his home many times between the spring of 1972 and mid-1979. Every visit was a celebration of good humor and spirited conversation. He encouraged me in the beginning to "hurry up and get that book built . . . people will love it."

In June of 1974 on the eve of the publication of **MOUNTAIN SPIRITS,** *Simmie had a message for the NBC television people in New York:*

"You tell 'em I watch the TODAY show every day and I think that Barbara Walters is as sharp as a split splinter!"

As the saying goes, they broke the mold with Simmie.

I mourn his passing and revere his memory.

J.E.D.

Chapter 2

Mountain Wines, Ciders and Beers

In the old days they ground apples up in a hand-cranked apple mill or put 'em in troughs. Beat 'em up into pomace and placed into barrel for fermentation. Sometimes they added sugar and sometimes a little bit of barley malt. Then, after fermentation, they put it in the still, capped it down and stilled it.

— Verner Fox

Mountain Wines, Ciders and Beers

It is a real treat to drive through the Appalachian hill country east of Ellijay, Georgia, in apple blossom time and sniff the magnificent aroma wafting across the countryside.

With the majestic Blue Ridge Mountain chain hovering on the horizon, hundreds of acres of apple trees stretch across the rolling plateau almost as far as the eye can see.

Yet in this same Gilmer County, Georgia's premier county for the production of apples, hard apple cider is difficult to find. The fact that the county is legally "dry" may have something to do with it.

Buck Carver of Dillard, Ga. holds tiny copper pot still he built.

While roadside stands advertise "apple cider," it is nothing like the pungent spirits of pioneer days such as that consumed by President John Adams at the rate of two tankards daily.

For the most part, what one finds is a rather weak imitation—apple juice with a bit of water added.

Hard cider making still goes on in the mountains, however, but it is mostly "made to drink, not to sell," as the local saying goes.

Reed Stanley, a jovial, ruddy-faced son of a pioneer north Georgia mountain family, remembers the plenteous days of hard cider barrels of it—on the family farm. Many mountain families kept a gourd dipper hung alongside the barrel as a hospitable welcome to friends and passersby.

"We used to make a whole lot of it at our farm at Big Creek on the Blue Ridge divide," remembered Reed. "And we gave it to everybody who lived around close. We didn't sell it.

"My dad really liked his cider. He always said it was good for your stomach. And he'd always make sassafras tea every spring and make us boys drink it."

Although Reed's father made corn whiskey—as did a great

Reed Stanley of Ellijay, Ga. He remembers brandy-making, and hard cider.

majority of his neighbors throughout the Appalachian foothills—
he abstained from drinking it. "No, my dad never did drink likker,"
said Reed. "I never did see none of my brothers high, either."

As to hard cider, here is how Reed Stanley remembers it being
made:

REAL APPLE CIDER*

"We made the cider at home. We had an old cider mill and
we'd grind up apples and make cider and we'd let it work about
seven days. We put five pounds of sugar on, say, two bushels of
crushed apples. That sugar'll just work the life out of that.

"We had a press. We'd grind these apples and put it in the press.
It had a handle on top and it would just press all the juice out.
Then we put it in a barrel and let it work. That juice would just
work and it would get sharp as a brar. We just let the juice work.
We didn't let the rest of the pomace in—like for brandy. If you put
five pounds of sugar to two bushels of apples, that made it, I mean,
really work.

"When it's workin', it gives off a fine bubble—works all over.
You can put your ear down there and hear it just a poppin'.

"It would work off in seven days. You could tell when it had
worked off. It would taste sharp. It would quit working. After so
long of a time, it would have one big bubble every once in a while.
That's a sour bubble.

"When it had worked off, you just seal it up. We'd put it in
barrels or in a crock. Dad always put his'n in a crock in a spring

---

*¹ Mrs. M.P. Porter (whose cook book was published in the late 1800's)
offered a special recipe for keeping cider sweet all winter. "Bruise one pound
of white mustard seed and add two eggs well beaten and one pint of fresh
milk. When the cider is in a condition for drinking, pour in the above mixture,
shake the barrel well and bung tightly. The cider can be consumed when it
settles."

*² Not all cider connoisseurs prefer the "hard" kind. Some like "Sweet"
or unfermented cider. To keep your cider sweet, as the juice accumulates in
the barrel, it should not be allowed to stand in warm weather for more than
one day. Then it should be sealed in the barrel. Turn the barrel every week
for five weeks, then draw off the clear cider into bottles and cork tightly.
Place in a wine cellar or any other suitable cold, dry place. The *Farmer's
Almanack* of 1839 gave this instruction for keeping cider sweet: "About a
one/half pint of mustard seed in a barrel of cider will keep it sweet through
the entire winter."

where it's cold. We had a spring house the water run through. We didn't have a frigidaire, and Dad had a big-old five gallon crock. Shouldn't seal it up; it'll build up pressure and blow up. It's fermated (sic) enough. I mean it's stout! Dad'd just tie a big white cloth over this crock. And that cider, the longer you keep it, the harder it gets and the sharper it gets."

MAUD THACKER

Maud Thacker was one of eight children who grew up in a one-room log cabin at the foot of Hendricks Mountain in Pickens County, Georgia. A tall, rangy daughter of the mountains with long pigtails trailing down her back, Maud was her father's tomboy favorite, and worked as hard as the boys, "Plowing a mule many of a day on that mountain from sunup to sundown," growing corn, peas, beans and potatoes, "shucking" the cows and feeding the mules and hogs every morning, even starting up the fire on winter mornings in the cabin's giant fireplace.

Maud worked hard in the woods, also, snaking out crosstie logs and cutting board timber from the side of the mountain. "You didn't have to drive those steers," she remembered. "You just talk to 'em and they'd go where you told 'em to."

And Maud learned plenty about making mountain spirits, rawhiding sacks of corn meal and malt on her back from the wagon down to the still, operated by her father, Eli Fields.

"Yeah," Maud said with a big grin, "I made apple brandy when I was a kid. Hope my daddy make it in a copper still, just like you make whiskey. We had a whole lot of apple trees. When the apples would get good and meller, we'd stir that mash and mix 'em up in a box and still 'em. Didn't add sugar."

Later in life, after she had gotten married and raised a family, Maud learned the art of winemaking, utilizing local muscadine grapes, blackberries, elderberries and dewberries. When I visited her, Maud had six kinds of wine—a veritable rainbow of fermented fruits—lining her refrigerator shelves. "Fer if anybody gets sick, I got what they need," she says. Many people do, indeed, come for Maud's wine, "to build up their blood."

Although Maud's mother and father never made wine, she learned it on her own. Once she had a quart of blackberries to spoil and she turned them into wine. Just sweetened them and worked them and turned them into wine. "They didn't make but just a taddle," she recalls. But she discovered the medicinal powers

Maud Thacker, wine maker supreme

Maud and Author

of wine when her son, then 43, had stomach trouble, "spitting up his vittles." Maud gave him that first batch of blackberry wine. It worked miracles, and settled his stomach. Ever since, Maud has kept home made wine on hand.

Maud's specialty is elderberry wine and she makes a lot of it, filling orders for people who come from miles around, because many believe elderberry wine is good for arthritis "to build up your blood."

ELDERBERRY WINE

Here is how Maud makes elderberry wine:

"I pick my elderberries up yonder on that mountain north of Jasper, on the road towards the monument. After you pick them off of them big bunches, the elderberries are just about the size of a bird's eye.

"I wash 'em good and put 'em in glass and gallon jugs, sometimes in a churn. I get them nearly filled with elderberries and then I put in the sugar. I don't measure the sugar. Just add it 'till it tastes right—sorta sweet, but not too sweet—and pour warm water over it and put a lid on it, but not tight. I just set the jars down there in the smokehouse and let them work. Sometimes it takes months to work off. But if you cook your berries out, it'll work off nearly in a month. I use three wine makers. When the mash quits bubbling, I know it's worked off. I strain the berries twice. I first strain them through a sifter, then when they work off, I strain them through a cloth. After it quits bubbling, I take it out and seal it in a jar and put it in the refrigerator."

MOUNTAIN BEER

One of the tastiest and most popular beverage spirits in the mountains—among mountain men, themselves—are the beers made from fruit and corn. Moonshiners, particularly, have been noted for drinking the "distiller's beer" from mash boxes. Many preferred this beer to the corn whiskey and brandies which were the product of later distillation.

Ironically, these beers seldom ever got bottled or consumed out of the woods, being a mere by-product of whisky-making.

A deceased Baptist preacher from Greenville County, South Carolina, who as a youngster served as a lookout for his brother's distillery in "the Dark Corner" of South Carolina, recalled to me

'Twas the 5th of December,
As well as I remember
I staggered into town in drunken pride

No one was I disturbin'
I lay down by the curbin'
A hog came up and lay down by my side.

Then two ladies came my way
And I overheard one say,

You can tell a man who's boozin'
By the company he chooses,

And the hog got up and slowly walked away.
— N.C. Mountain doggerel (anon)

how he sipped distiller's beer from his brother's mash barrels.

"It was one of our little self-adventures," the preacher remembered. "After they mixed the malt with the corn meal and water, that fermented and made beer. We used to love to drink that beer. There was a little weed that grew around the edges of the bottom land. It was hollow. We'd cut that down and stick it in that beer and drink it up through that."

Donald L. McCourry, a self-educated young newspaper writer from Dog Flat Hollow, North Carolina, remembers well how his folks made home brew.

"We would spirit corn in a tobacco bed cloth, place it in the ground, and cover it with dirt. We beat up the corn with a hammer, then put the meal with some mill-ground meal into a tub and sweetened it. After it set up for about four days, it would sour, then strain out and be ready to drink." Although it apparently was a right tasty beverage, Donald never drank more than a "sup," he said.

The Creek Indians of the Southeast had a special corn beer, *Sagamite*, which was very popular as a beverage during the Revolutionary War period and, most likely, before. Frenchman Louis LeClerc Milford, who lived for two decades with the Creeks in

West Georgia and Alabama beginning in 1775, said *Sagamite* was "a fermentation of corn meal, which, after having been boiled, retains a rather pleasant ciderlike taste."

While corn beer was well liked by Appalachian moonshiners, their favorite was the mash fermented to make apple and peach beer.

PEACH BEER

"Yes, sir," said Thee King, the noted still-tender at the Georgia Mountain Fair, Hiawassee, Georgia, "that peach beer is pretty tasty stuff when it's worked off. Delicious. Best drink in the world. Lotta times, we'd drink it from the barrel. We used to have an old holler weed we called Queen of the Meader (meadow). Find them around old swamps. Anywhere there was water, where a branch run down through the mountains. Those weeds would grow up, get higher than your head. Cut 'em down and they are holler, you know, and suck the beer through that. We'd like to go in to the still to get in the wood ready for a run say like tonight. We'd always have to sample that beer, because it was right ready!"

Cider making on Long Island from a painting by William M. Davis. Painted in 1871. (Courtesy of the New York State Historical Association, Cooperstown, N.Y.)

Buck Carver of Rabun County, Georgia, on the other side of the Blue Ridge mountains, also attests to the flavor and popularity of fruit beer, which he sipped through the hollow weeds that he called "bugle weed."* "Ah, that peach beer, we loved it. Drink it in the woods from the mash barrels. Get as drunk as a fiddler's fice (dog). Yes, sir. When it gets just about ready to run (distill), by Ned, it'll knock your pillars out from under you."

But here again, the beer was just a by-product of the main objective . . . that of making brandy or whiskey. As a result, little of it has ever made it out of the woods.

To make peach beer, though, you take the same fermentation steps as in making brandy. Except that you don't distill it. You have to drink it then, or put it in a refrigerator. Here is Buck's description of how peach beer is made:

"Well, the more rotten your peaches, the better. If they're half rotten when you load 'em up and haul 'em to the woods, that's just fine. You want to get all them kernels (seed) out of there. If you don't remove the kernels, and if you should go on and distill it into brandy, it'll have the bitterest whang. Yes, sir, squeeze them seeds out of her. Some people take a close mesh wire on a pole to dip the seeds out. If a feller wants to get all the seeds out, though, he'll take them out by hand before he throws the peach meat into the barrel. I always done it with my hands. Your hands will be so sore the skin will break open. Hell fire, the skin will be so weak you can't even scratch your head, much less your hind end.

"Atter you get the kernels out, put the peaches in a barrel and let it set there until it rots. Lot of people churn 'em up and down. Best to get down barefooted (in the barrel) like any other nigger would and just stomp up and down.

"Let that set about 72 hours or so, souring. Then throw you a little sweetening compound on there. You'll mash about seven bushels of peaches to the (50-gallon) barrel. On the first round, we'd put about 40/50 pounds of sugar. There's a right smart more sugar in peaches than they are in apples.

"When your bubbling ceases and fermentation has ended, we'd take some screen wire and strain that peach beer over into a bucket. Now you talk about pigs in a bucket, we lapped her up."

*Buck said mountain people would cut bugle weeds and use them as whistles. "We'd cut one shorter than the other and put it in your mouth and blow. Sound like a double train whistle."

PERSIMMON BEER

Among the fermented fruit spirits, one of the old-timey mountain favorites is that of persimmon beer. Louise and Bil Dwyer* of Highlands, North Carolina, remember the time when persimmon beer served as a substitute for milk when a family's cow "went dry." This was made by fermenting well-ripened persimmons, apple cores and peelings.

TOMATO BEER

Still another unusual yet apparently very popular drink in the Appalachians was tomato beer. Mrs. M.E. Porter included the recipe in her *New Southern Cookery Book* which was published shortly after the Civil War. It was re-issued in 1974 by Promontory Press. This was her recipe:

"Wash and mash ripe tomatoes and strain them through a coarse linen bag. To every gallon of juice, add three pounds of brown sugar. Let stand nine days, then pour it off from the pulp which has settled to the bottom. Bottle and cover tightly. The longer you keep it, the better it gets. When ready to drink, add a half-tumblerful of beer to a gallon of cold, sweetened water. Add a few drops of lemon extract, if available."

SCUPPERNONG WINE

Here is a widely used southern recipe for scuppernong wine:

Place five gallons of slightly rotten grapes in a large crock. Mash them up with a potato masher. Pour one and one-quarter gallons of boiling water and let stand one day and night.

Pour off the juice, using a fine-mesh strain. Add 12 pounds of sugar, and stir thoroughly. Let this stand for one day and one night. Skim off the scum from top, strain the mixture and place in one-gallon, open mouth plastic containers. Cover each with a thin cloth. Every few days, take a large spoon and clean skimmings off the top. Let this stand for about two months, at which time it should be ready for bottling. Give wine a final straining through cloth, bottle and cork. In one month, it will be ready for use, but the longer it ages, the better.

*In their book, *Appalachian Mountain Country Cookin'*.

Earl Palmer

Private Enterprise:
Bushrod Cockram does not run off the most corn likker on Raven's Den Creek. But, like he tells it: "When my mash works off just right, I can get me two cases of twelve halves of single-foot likker a run from the 120-gallon, copper-bottomed sub outfit of mine, then slop back for another run th' same night. Who this side of hell can fault a feller for having a business of his own to raise up his family," he inquired, and he hammered one fist into its mate to drive his words home.

PUMPKIN GIN

While on the subject of home-made wines, perhaps it would be worthwhile to list the recipe for "pumpkin gin" offered on the floor of the United States Senate by Missouri Senator James A. Reed. A former mayor of Kansas City, Reed's recipe was offered during the height of National Prohibition (1919-1933):

Pluck a ripe pumpkin, cut a plug out of the top and clean out the seeds. Fill it with sugar and seal the plug with parafin. Open up in 30 days and pour out the wine.

GRAPE WINE

Mrs. Roy Brumit of East Tennessee offers the following recipe for grape wine:

Mash 60 cups of grapes in a stone crock. Add five quarts of boiling water, cover and let stand for three days. Strain through a cheesecloth. Add 10 cups of sugar and a whole egg in shell. Cover and let stand until it is fermented. which will take about three weeks. Skim periodically and strain several times. It is time to strain it and bottle it when the egg goes to the bottom of the crock.

MEAD

Since honey has been one of the most abundant "fruits" of the mountains—with practically every settler either having his own "bee gums" (hives) or being able to rob the wild honey from the trees—mead and its more basic companion beverage, methaglin, found great popularity in the Appalachians from frontier days.

The honey/water wine has been celebrated as a fermented beverage from ancient Greece and Rome and was popular in Europe in the Middle Ages. Although the making of mead has almost disappeared from the Appalachians, here is a recipe handed down from frontier days:

> Two quarts honey
> Five gallons of rainwater
> One cup rose water
> A dozen cinnamon sticks, pulverized
> Two cloves
> Two teaspoons nutmeg, grated

Place all ingredients, except for the rose water, in a container, making sure to thoroughly crush the spices. Mix the honey, water and spices thoroughly. Place in a big pot or kettle and boil for an hour, or until the froth disappears from the top. Pour the mixture into a barrel and place it in a warm place with only a thin cloth over the open bung hole to keep out flies, insects and dust. Fermentation takes one to two weeks, depending on the temperature. Skim off the foam daily and add more honey and water. When the mixture stops fermenting (bubbling), seal up the barrel (drive in the bung) and let stand for a month. Then draw the mead into bottles and cork. The bottles should be stored in a dry, dark and cool place such as a wine cellar.

PARSNIP WINE

The best time of the year to make Parsnip wine, according to Mrs. R.G. Regan of Glade Spring, Virginia, is in February. That is the month you should take the parsnips out of the ground to obtain the right wine flavor.

Here is her recipe, as included in the booklet, *Old Timey Recipes*, collected and published by Phyllis Connor of Bluefield, West Virginia:

> 1 quart grated parsnips
> 1 gallon boiling water
> 2½ pounds white sugar
> 2/4 teacup liquid yeast

Put grated parsnips in a stone jar. Pour boiling water over them. Set jar on back of stove where it will keep hot, but will not boil. Leave it there four hours, Strain. Wash jar, then return to the liquid to it. Add sugar, stir until dissolved. When lukewarm, add yeast. Let stand until seasoned.

RHUBARB WINE

I am indebted to Gertrude Harris, author of *Foods of the Frontier*,* for the recipe to this beverage, which she reports was very popular on all frontiers, "for the hardy rhubarb plant—known as pie-plant and wine-plant, grew almost everywhere." The familiar pie plant could be found near the kitchen door of many abandoned

*From *Foods of the Frontier*, published 1972 by 101 Productions, San Francisco.

"Proofin'-down." Man in center of picture is adding weak-proof "backins" to high-proof "first-shots" to bring the whiskey to what is called "proof-strength." This is around 80 proof, visual, of course, and is average proof of good grade moonshine whiskey.

Earl Palmer

cabins, and many women, when they moved further west, carried the "crown" of the rhubarb plant for planting at their new home. Only the stalk is used since the leaves and root are poisonous.

4 pounds rhubarb (about 14 stalks)
1 gallon boiling water
1 teaspoon shredded ginger (fresh or dried)
4 pounds sugar
½ yeast cake
¾ tablespoon unflavored gelatin, dissolved
    in ½ cup water

Wash rhubarb well and cut off leaf and root flares. Cut into small dice and put into stoneware crock. Add the boiling water and ginger. Set aside for three days, then strain through double

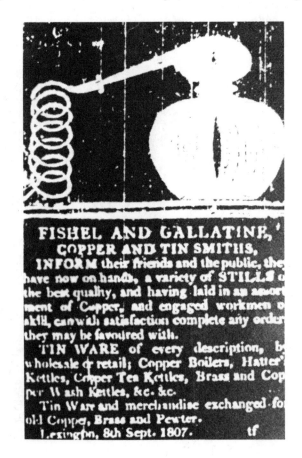

FISHEL AND GALLATINE,
COPPER AND TIN SMITHS,
INFORM their friends and the public, they have now on hands, a variety of STILLS of the best quality, and having laid in an assortment of Copper, and engaged workmen of skill, can with satisfaction complete any order they may be favoured with.
TIN WARE of every description, by wholesale or retail; Copper Boilers, Hatter's Kettles, Copper Tea Kettles, Brass and Copper Wash Kettles, &c. &c.
Tin Ware and merchandise exchanged for old Copper, Brass and Pewter.
Lexington, 8th Sept. 1807.   tf

cheesecloth. Add the sugar and yeast, then the liquid gelatin. Let stand for two more days. Then pour into a large jug and cork tightly. Set aside in a cool dark place for at least three months, then strain carefully and pour into bottles and cork. Lay on sides as usual with all wine bottles. The wine is now ready to drink.

CHERRY BOUNCE

This has been a favorite drink among people of the Appalachian South since pioneer days. One of the most famous concocters of this drink prior to and following the Civil War was Amos Owens of Cherry Mountain, North Carolina, in the foothills east of Asheville. A jovial, rotund whisky maker of the old school, Amos was known widely as "the cherry bounce king." It was said that his bounce would give a person strength enough to "whip this here depression single-handed." Owens' biographer didn't give an exact recipe for Amos' cherry bounce, but said it was a mixture of his copper-pot-distilled corn whiskey, sourwood honey and juice from the big, black-heart cherries he grew on his mountain. Owens' daughters crushed the cherries by stomping them with their bare feet.

In later years, this recipe emerged, and was published by the Junior Service League of Johnson City, Tennessee, in its book, *Smoky Mountain Magic*:

"To one gallon of white whiskey, put two quarts of water and five to six quarts of wild cherries. Cover tightly and let stand for three months. Drain off the liquor and strain well, sometimes twice. Make a thick syrup with one and one-half pounds white sugar and water. Boil until ropy. Add the syrup to the liquor according to taste."

SASSAFRAS TEA

Sassafras Tea, of cource, is not a spirit beverage. But since it is so strongly identified with the mountains, and mountain people, perhaps it is worthwhile to list as the finale in this chapter.

The drinking of sassafras tea has long been a spring-time tradition among the people of the Appalachians, serving as an invigorating tonic and an antidote to spring fever.

Reed Stanley remembers his father always drank sassafras tea in the spring to thin his blood. And he insisted that his sons drink it, also:

"Dad would always in the spring of the year, when the sap

began to rise and then warm days started coming, he'd make us get out and dig sassafras roots out of the ground and wash 'em right real good. And he boiled them things and made us drink it and he drunk it."

It was just the tonic, Reed said, to get a person started off in the springtime, thinning the blood, enabling one to work in the hot fields after a long winter when the blood was thickened.

Here is the recipe for sassafras tea:

Place four cups of water in a pot and bring it to boiling. Add two pieces of sassafras about three inches long. Cover and let it simmer for about a half hour. Add a little sugar and serve it piping hot.

'Twas honest old Noah first planted the Vine
And mended his Morals by drinking its Wine;
He justly the drinking of Water decry'd;
For he knew that all Mankind, by drinking it, dy'd.
— Benjamin Franklin

Chapter
3

Brandy:
Southern Birthright

The manufacture of spirits, first a domestic handicraft like weaving, blacksmithing, tanning and candle-making; then a small-scale vocation, usually associated with milling and farming; then a family profession, well supplied with secret formulas . . . .
— *H.F. Willkie,*
Beverage Spirits in America

Brandy:
Southern Birthright

Ever hear of "split brandy?" Or apple/syrup brandy? They are part and parcel of the spirits vocabulary of the Southern Appalachians, just as are apple, plum, peach and blackberry brandy. And most "pure brandy" bought in the hills since the turn of the century has been "split"—that is, split between the fruit mash and grain mash. With a bit of sugar, honey or molasses thrown in to help it "work."

"Only one kind of brandy I tried to make and failed," said my one-time-moonshiner friend, Thee King, a lanky, Linconesque-looking mountaineer of Hiawassee, Georgia. "That was roastn'ear brandy. We just put up one barrel, but I never could get it to by-God bead."

Thee even went so far one time as to make raisin brandy. "Raisinjack, I guess you would call it. A merchant in Hiawassee got a barrel of raisins . . . sell 'em by the pound in a scoop. Got worms in it and he wanted us to work 'em off."

As Thee King describes it, pure brandy "is just usin' apples, plums, grapes, elderberries, maypops or whatever. You don't put no sugar a'tall in 'em. Just use rye malt, sprouted rye, distill the wine and then you got pure damn brandy. But we always put anyhow 25 pounds of sugar to the barrel."

Earl Palmer

Brandy "run"—"Flake stand" (condenser) spews out a "run" of "apple-flat" brandy. And the quality is good, the still being charged with pure apple "pummies," with relatively little sugar being added to the mash. Pure, "straight brandy" is virtually passe. Moonshiners, generally, "temper" their brandy with a "single foot" whiskey. The novice buyer is not qui-vive to this ages old artifice, but bootleggers buying for resale know the difference and thus are sold what the moonshiner labels "pure brandy" even though sugar is added to the "pummies." Scarcity of pure apple or peach brandy can be predicated on the fact that mash boxes are tied up for four weeks while a batch of "pummies" "works off." Oldtimers get $40 or more for a gallon of brandy of around 125 proof and boasting the aroma of an apple house late in the fall.

There were stills on most of the large plantations and
apples and peaches were turned into brandy, which was
drunk moderately and thankfully. Everybody drank in those
days (1800's) except a few very strict Methodists.
> — *Rev. George Gillman Smith,*
> *"The Story of Georgia and*
> *the Georgia People."*

Many mountain people like King declare the making of brandy is similar in most respects to manufacturing whiskey. One old timer told me: "Ain't no difference in making brandy, corn whiskey, moonshine. All come under the same headin'."

But Thee King—well experienced in trying out all mountain spirits—is not impressed by the taste of brandy. "I never did see anything special about brandy. Smells good. But I'll just tell you the truth about it. I don't like it. It's too faarry . . . ."

"It's powerful stuff if it's made right," declared Verner Fox of Dial, Georgia. "It's fiery and too acidy for drinking. Now it smells good. I like to smell it. Smells like crabapple in the woods. But you put it on a varnish surface and it will take the varnish off!"

A young brandy maker from Cartecay, Georgia, declares: "Just anybody can't afford brandy. Mostly for judges and lawyers!" (At $40 a gallon, it's understandable why).

Connoisseurs inexperienced in drinking Appalachian brandies are often surprised when they take their first nip. Even whiskey men. A moonshiner in Sugar Valley, Georgia, accustomed to drinking corn whiskey straight, remembers his traumatic introduction:

"My uncle drove up in his pickup and it smelled like rotten apples. He had some apple brandy and offered me some. I looked at that half gallon jar of clear apple brandy. Looked just like moonshine. I just sloshed it around a time or two and took a big gulp. DAMN, I MUST HAVE FARTED FIRE!"

Over the years, among the mountain people themselves, brandy's main purpose was to provide a base for medicine. "Any of these doctors will tell you that brandy and honey is the healinest things to lungs they's ever been," said Reed Stanley, an enterprising Ellijay, Georgia motelman. "It's the best cough syrup ever made."

When he was making brandy in the 1930's, all of his brandy customers used it for medicine. "I'd usually leave my brandy at 140 proof, and I'd take it and put it in two demijohns, a half gallon in each one. Every one of these old mountaineers had mountain honey and they'd fill them jugs up . . . a half a gallon of brandy and a half a gallon of honey in each jug. And that's what they used for kids as cough syrup. Best cough syrup ever made."

In making apple brandy in the old days, mountain people would crush their apples in a hollowed out log; later they went to hand-cranked cider mills.

The late Peg Fields of Jasper, Georgia, told me about the old way. "They'd get a big poplar log, about 24 inches through. Take a foot adz and dig a big enough of a trough to pour four or five bushels of apples in it. They'd put it up on legs, two on each end. You'd take a small maul, a mallet, and beat the apples up. One end

Thee King builds a still, encased in rock furnace.

Earl Palmer

Mountain Coffee Pot:
Like hoss collars and monkey wrenches, whiskey stills come in all sizes. This
little feller, a "solid copper" outfit, can turn out better drinkin' likker, can be
concealed in a single laurel bush from the all-seeing eyes of "th' law." In fact
it's possible to walk within twenty-five yards of such a tiny "mountain coffee
pot" and not be aware of its presence if an expert fireman is in the shack.
And, let it be tattled, most mountain whiskey men are master fire-builders.
Though a small colt as stills go, by "slopping back," an output of 8-10 gallons
of singlefoot can be turned out between two suns.

would be higher and that juice would run down to the end. Then you'd rake your beat apples down and put them in the barrel, too. When they had the beaten apples and juice in the barrel, they'd put the head back on the barrel, and the hoops back down on it. Seal that up with dried meal and red clay. Seal it up air tight. They put them brandy pummies in a building. Leave the pummies there all winter. It would go into a complete rot in the winter. When it got warm the next spring. they'd take the top end off and it would start working. They didn't have no sugar to put on. Made straight brandy."

Fields, who learned his whiskey-making and brandy making from his father, Eli, would laugh when he heard people talk about "pure apple brandy," that is, brandy made without sugar.

"Nowadays you can't get no brandy that has no sugar on it. If anybody tells you that they got some brandy that ain't got no sugar on it, if he ain't too big, you just tell him he's a damn liar."

One brandy maker told me that if a person wishes to make a good grade brandy, he should not put over 10 pounds of sugar in a 55-gallon barrel of mash. The more sugar put in, of course, the more brandy you make, but excessive sugar can reduce the quality of the turnout substantially.

Although the price of brandy in the mountains runs upwards to $40 a gallon, it is very difficult to find. One of Reed Stanley's brandy customers of decades ago visited him in 1975 seeking a bit of apple brandy for medicine. "We spent a week hunting brandy," said Reed, "and we didn't find a drop."

Of all mountain brandies, apple brandy is the most popular by far, but you get many opinions as to which apples are the best to use. Thee King goes for "hog sweets," Simmie Free likes "streaked Junes," while a young applejack aficionado from Elli-jay, Georgia, prefers "golden delicious." It all depends on whether you want a sour apple, with a lot of acid in it, or a sweet apple such as golden delicious, with more sugar in it.

Here are three apple brandy recipes from three colorful mountain men. We will lead off with the aforementioned Thee King, who likes to be called "doctor" because he dispenses so much "mountain medicine."

HOG SWEET APPLE BRANDY

"The best brandy in the world," says King, "is made from hog sweet apples. Used to be plenty of them in this county. It's a white early apple. First the June apples come in, and Early Harvest. Then Hog Sweets come in next. We had about six or eight trees over at home (at Hiawassee, Georgia), *and they would yield!* We had a cider mill. Grind them durn things up. Boy, I dreaded it. Turned the thing by hand. Put up about 20 to 40 barrels of pomace. We also beat 'em up with a maul, in a trough. I beat many a day and night of them sons-of-a-gun.

"You take your apple pomace and scald the piss out of 'em with hot scalding water. They're just as good. Just get 'em where they'll sour. You let your pomace rot four days, sometimes six or eight depending on the water. When you break 'em up, you add sugar (25 pounds) and meal (one peck). You've got to stir it up good, like this morning. Then the next morning, stir 'em up again. It'll push up there a big cap. We have used rye meal to cap 'em. But there's no need for that. Sours 'em quicker. Then you go back. You can tell when it's ready. Take your hand and run through (the pomace). When it quits foaming and clears off, you can 'run' it."

We were 'born into brandy. The whole county bounded
in large orchards. Upon almost every farm there was a
distillery. Brandy was drunk at births by the suffering
mother, the midwife and the gossips who attended. The
lips of the infant were moistened with a weak beverage.

— George W. Pascal, In Ninety-
Four Years, published 1871
in Washington, Georgia

STREAKED JUNE APPLE BRANDY

As mentioned previously, Simmie Free of Rabun County, Georgia, preferred to make his brandy out of Streaked June Apples.

"There's a difference in apples," said Simmie. "Some use as much again (sugar) as others. I know why, they're sour. I got four trees I set out, purpose to make brandy out of. Streaked June. They take more sugar than Delicious. On Streaked Junes, you have to use 50 pounds of sugar to the (55-gallon) barrel, where you'd use only 25 with Delicious."

Here's how Simmie made his brandy from Streaked Junes:

"What you do after you've gathered your apples, you get a maul and beat 'em up. You get a better turn-out when you beat

The Late Peg Fields

'em. Get a better taste of brandy, but don't run (distill) it too soon. You've got to wait 'til it gets ready and then make it. And then you've got a mild taste and its strong as the dickens, too. Makes you want to just keep drinkin' it. After awhile you'll be layin' down, wantin' to move, and can't. Yeah, that brandy'll knock your eyes out, if you ain't used to it.

"I used to beat lots of 'um. You can get you a good long hickory pole and make you a maul on the end. Get you somethin' to beat 'em in. You can just set in a chair and just beat the devil out of 'em. That there hickory pole will come back up every time. You don't have to pull it up. When you get your beater full, pour it over in the barrel. Put the pomace in (55-gallon) wooden barrels. Not in those old iron drums. Use wooden.

"Pour in the pomace about eight inches deep in the barrel. Then get you some good home made rye (meal) and just sprinkle it like you're puttin' face powders on it. Then the next batch do do the same thing. Until you've got your barrel two-thirds full. That's all you can get in a 50-or-60-gallon still. And then when you beat the lastun's up, don't put nothin' on it. Just let it set there 'til the next morning. Go then and put your water on it, a quart of malt and sugar—on Streaked Junes you'll have to use 50 pounds of sugar—and stir it up real good. Course you don't want to put *too* much sugar in your pummie. Not too much on brandy.

"Then you go ahead and put water on 'em. Stir 'em up good and then the last thing you do, you put a quart of rye—not over a quart of rye at the biggest.

"Now workin' off. It depends on the weather. I always put mine in a building and let it work off and when they got ready, take my mule and sled 'em out to (the still) when I'm going to run 'em.

"When it's ready, it tastes bitter. You think, 'Well, that ain't going to do no good. But that's where the power is. Then you run it. Ah, it'd be way up yonder, higher than I could tell. Way above a hundred, as high as White Lightnin'.

"Temper it with water. Take a third water to make it come to sort of a bead. Then it would pass for a hundred.

"Out of a 55-gallon barrel, you get 10 to 11 gallons (of brandy). High falutin' stuff. *Plum good.* I'll tell you what it'd do. Everybody'd like it."

APPLE/SYRUP BRANDY

John Henry Chumley was 89 years old when I interviewed him last at his home hear Dawsonville, Georgia. His memory was crystal clear.

"In my day back near the Amicalola River in Dawson County, I had a neighbor who had a big apple orchard. He had a cider mill and he'd grind 'em apples up and pour 'em up in 50-gallon barrels and pour enough of the cider in to come to the top.

"Then he'd lay a lid over 'em down there on the branch. Let 'em stay there about two/three weeks. After they'd get good and rotten, he'd put about eight to ten gallons of syrup to the barrel. Boy! She'd turn to brandy, and we'd sell it for staight brandy after we got it stilled.

"Lord, it'd make it. We stilled it, me and Oz Brady. It'd work off after we put that syrup in there, you know, and it'd just roar. Then it'd sink down about that fer (five, six inches). It was ready to run and we'd slip around, me and Oz Brady, we had two copper stills, and we'd make the brandy. P'shaw! It'd make over a gallon to the gallon of syrup that you put on. Pure old brandy. And it'uz high. That was along 'fore that first world war. It got up to where it was $10 a gallon.

POWELL STILL—This still belonged to Dr. Chapman Powell, who had a log cabin on the Shallowford Indian Trail (now Clairmont Road) when he was also sheriff of DeKalb County, Georgia, in 1833. In this cabin (now at Stone Mountain Park), Dr. Powell treated settlers and Indians with his corn whiskey medicine and his cabin was called "The Medicine House." His medicine was a gallon of whiskey in which he mixed herbs and pulverized roots. This turnip type "medicine still" is now on display in Decatur, Ga., in the DeKalb Historical Society Museum (old courthouse). Here it is viewed by Beth Heist. Still was built in 1800s. (Photo by Charles Pugh).

"That syrup. My daddy, old man Jack Chumley, had a big syrup mill out there in the county and we made syrup all the time. Me and my brother run the syrup box. My daddy was getting pretty old then. Brother Charlie fed the mill with cane. We'd make four and five and 600 gallons a year. You know, people hauling the cane in. I seed my daddy sell Bob S. (a big whiskey maker) 300 gallons of syrup for a thousand dollars. Bob said he got over $3,000 out of that syrup liquor and mashed corn meal.

"After he run the first run of straight corn, then on the pot tail, he'd put syrup on it and it'd work off . . . make over a gallon of whiskey to the gallon of syrup. And he'd get $10 for every bit of likker you could get. It was durin' the time of that (world) war. Sugar was not available. There was lots of likker-making then and the law didn't fool with it. They didn't fool with nobody. Didn't hardly ever hear of a still gettin' cut nowheres. Nearly all the young men in the county was in the army.

"Peaches made just as good. Trouble with peaches, there was no way in the world to grind 'em on the cider mill. You just had to let 'em rot. So the seeds woudn't clog up the mill.

PEACH BRANDY

Second in popularity to apple brandy is peach brandy. Many connoisseurs rate peach brandy tops, preferring its milder taste. Virtually all of the mountain makers of apple brandy also have experience in making peach brandy. Here is a recipe offered me by a young man from Cartecay, Georgia, who wishes not to be identified:

"You just put your peaches in a barrel and straighten out a hoe and chop them four or five times. In about four days, they'll just turn to water. Go all to pieces. Just like water in a barrel. So you don't have to add water. You can dip it off then and pour your bunkers (seeds) out.

"The pomace is sweet for only two weeks. Then it turns real bitter. Turns sour and smells just like alcohol. Make you drunk to smell it, nearly. It turns sort of dark cast after it sets awhile.

"Then you still it. Don't age it. Just put it in jars. Seems like it don't smell like brandy for two/three weeks. Then, after a month, it'll really get to smelling. If you let it set in the woods, it's so strong the acid will eat the caps off. I guess that's why it burns people up to drink it."

Here is Thee King's recipe for peach brandy:

"Way we used to do peach brandy, way back yonder in my younger days, we had plenty of peaches of our own. Trees around the house. We'd go to the orchard and packing houses and get 'em when they was rotten. Got to let 'em rot anyhow, to make brandy. Get an average run of peaches. Take hot water and scald 'em. Best thing to do is let 'em set in a barrel and rot, a week or ten days. Then you put in your malt and sugar.

"Peck of malt? You guessed it right on the button. Peck of malt to the barrel.

"Sugar. Seventy-five pounds if you was going to make it to sell. You ain't supposed to put any sugar if you're going to make pure brandy. But we put 25 pounds to the barrel. Then you'll put in four bushels of peaches.

"Let that set. It'll work off in 72 hours. You'll get a case of brandy . . . six gallons, when you still it. About a gallon and a half to the bushel. If it was pure brandy, with no sugar, you'd be lucky to get a gallon of brandy to the bushel."

SPLIT BRANDY

A jolly, rolly poly man, a Santa Claus in overalls, is Buck Carver of Rabun County, Georgia. Buck became one of my dearest friends and informants when I was researching my original book, *MOUNTAIN SPIRITS*. Buck is now a U.S. Forest Service employee, working in the vast Chattahoochee National Forest which was formerly his haunt in whiskey making. Here are Buck's comments on "split brandy."

"We made 'split brandy' right along, with corn whiskey. Here's how we made it:

"Wash your fruit and put it in a 50-gallon barrel. Lots of people churn it up and down with a straightened out hoe. Let it set for 72 hours or so, souring. Then add about 20 pounds of sugar.

"Now about the sugar. Of course, if you add sugar, that means you won't have pure brandy. But people will swear it's pure. Even

The moon shines east
And the moon shines west
But the man next door
Makes the moonshine best.
(anon)

old-timers, they'll swear up and down it's pure brandy and a knowin' better. The drinker won't know the difference if you don't sugar it too heavy.

"About 72 hours from the time you mash it in, your pomace starts breaking. When the bubbling stops and the beer is right sour, it's time to distill. Run it as quickly as possible.

"Now to make you some good brandy, on your next run, take the slop from your pot and add about a half bushel of corn meal to the barrel. Mix it in with your fruit pomace. That makes you some 'split brandy.'

"On that second run, let it sour for four or five days. Add a peck to a half bushel of corn meal and a half gallon of rye malt.

"Now that's 'split brandy.' The amazing thing, we couldn't convince nobody that it wasn't pure brandy. We'd say, 'We don't have any brandy but here's some split brandy.' They'd say, 'Don't tell me that ain't brandy. Hell fire, I've drunk too much of it; that's the real McCoy.' You'd try to tell them the truth of it, but they wouldn't have it. Lot of 'em wouldn't.

"We wouldn't think about leaving it at anything less than 115 proof.

"Most of our brandy went over to North Carolina. Bryson City. That brandy me and Neel made up there on Dover Gap— why you could get all the whiskey you wanted then for 25 cents a pint. A man who'd come and buy a quart for 50 cents, you'd invite him to Sunday dinner. Whiskey would wholesale for a dollar a gallon and brandy, $4.

"Last I made over on Kelley's creek, been about 16 years ago, I got $60 and $75 a case . . . $10 a gallon and more. I know of some being made now. On the State of Persimmon. But it's hard to find."

Both of the following recipes, for crabapple brandy and plum brandy, are a type of brandy/whiskey known by many mountain people as "split brandy."

CRABAPPLE BRANDY

For this recipe, I contacted my ex-moonshiner friend of Laughingal, Georgia, Hubert Howell. A lusty outdoorsman of many talents, Hubert likes to go barefooted all summer long. He has had a checkered career . . . farmer, cattleman, logger, moonshiner, bus driver, service station operator, and expert gardener. At

John Henry Chumley, 94, of Dawson County, Georgia, stands beside the old covered bridge which his father helped build in the 1800s, which crossed the Amicalola River. Mr. Chumley during his youth made whiskey and brandy farther up on the Amicalola River, near the Amicoloxia Falls, a Georgia state park. Mr. Chumley was for many years resident caretaker of the woodlands along the river for the Georgia Marble Company. The covered bridge, incidentally, burned to the ground in 1978, a victim of apparent arson.

age 78, Hubert is a sprightly, free-spirited farmer and gardener and his recollections of whiskey/brandy-making are vivid and clear.

"Now crabapple brandy, that was the *best smelling* stuff. You could smell that dog-gone stuff . . . oooooooo . . . all over the woods. Smell better than the blossoms. You could smell it a long way.

"Course, we always made our brandy along with corn whiskey. So it really wasn't pure brandy. We'd cook in a bushel of corn meal in a box, using hot pot tails from a previous run of corn whiskey. Cook that meal in with boiling water. Then we'd break that up . . . solid stuff looked like a piece of corn bread. We'd take a mash stick and cut that *all* to pieces—fill the box full of water- and get ever lump busted up. Then we'd put a two-peck bucket full of barley malt and a one-pound block of yeast in there. It'd start working pretty quick. When that worked down about 12 hours, then we'd put in the fruit, in this case, the beat-up crab-apples. We'd just pick up the crabapples about this time of year (late November) and grind them up.

"People loved it. They'd buy this half-brandy in preference to straight whiskey, this brandy with sugar in it. People couldn't tell the difference. We'd get $40 for the 10 gallons (in early 1930's) rather than $20 for whiskey.

"Now that crabapple brandy, when we sold it, it really had a good smell. You open up a bottle of it and it smelled *so* good . . . beter than any perfume. yeah. It smelt *good*!"

PLUM BRANDY (CUMBERLAND PLATEAU STYLE)

This recipe was offered by a friend who lives near Monteagle, Tennessee, on the Cumberland Plateau. True, it's plum brandy, but in exact terms, it's a combination of plum brandy and corn whiskey—a type of "split brandy" such as the crabapple brandy recipe offered by Hubert Howell, and a type of brandy/whiskey mountain people are famous for.

"Fill a 60-gallon barrel with crushed plums. The plums must be seeded.* Let set for three weeks, then mash up real good. Let work off about six weeks.

"On the first run, cook in one-half bushel of corn meal. Let cool. Then put in one gallon of corn malt. Distill.

---

*If the plums are not seeded (extracted from fruit), the seeds will clog up the still pipes and cause a blowup, our informant states.

Taft Densmore of Amicalola Falls, Georgia, remembers storing apple pummie by for winter. "Hit takes two weeks to a month to ferment apple pomace," says Taft. "Old timers would beat apples up in November and December and just let 'em set thar and run 'em and make brandy in the Spring. They'd put the pomace in a barrel, put some straw of pine needles on top of 'em and seal it up with three-quarters inches of red mud and leave it all winter. Put it in a shed somewheres. Back in them old days they used copper pots altogether, too. I put up a still right down yander one time and I used three worms. Had three worm boxes, one settin' right on top of the other. Had it underground. Shelter was lying on top of the ground and brush and leaves on top of it. An old cow fell in on it one time."

"On second and third runs, add 20 pounds of sugar and one gallon of malt to the leftover mash from the first and second runs. Also add a small amount of water. This recipe is good for all fruits as well as plums."

BLACKBERRY BRANDY

This is not a recipe for making blackberry brandy, only one mountain man's reaction to drinking a bit of it.

"It's a faary drink," he said. "We were down at the CCC Camp at Six, Georgia . . . me and four others shootin' out that ditch line. Some of the boys picked blackberries and made brandy. One of the fellers says, 'If you boys furnish me the money, I'll get us a quart of blackberry brandy.' You talk about somethin' potent. Oh! My gosh! That stuff'll put your moccasins a sunnin' in a hurry. We all drunk it. Got just as high as a Georgia pine. Feelin' no pain whatever.

"We put the brandy in bat wing pint bottles and drank the rest of it. We got just as high as a cat's back off that stuff and stayed that way all evening. When we went in to camp that night, we went to one of the lockers and waded into that other pint. We didn't make it to the mess hall that night. They had to bring us a sandwich to the tent. You talk about a case of the limber legs,

Apple brandy:
As contrasted with grain, straight corn, or sour mash, apple brandy sports the best "bloom," or "bead," holding it's head the longest. When the "bead" congregates in the center of a jug after mild shaking and is reluctant to "flash" off to the outer circle of the jug, and even then, floats high above the surface of pinto bean size, you can bet your last nickel that the "proof" is high, perhaps around 125-150, give or take a proof or so. A knowledgeable buyer can "read" the proof by pouring a small quantity in his palm, rub his hands briskly and then take a whiff.

Earl Palmer

now I mean we had it. That was the most powerful stuff. I believe to my soul it was every bit 150 proof . . . ."

HOW BRANDY IS MADE TODAY

Most of the recipes listed previously have gone into the way brandies were made in the old days. Here, to wrap up this chapter, is an interview I conducted with a 20-year-old in Gilmer County—Georgia's premier apple basket which is the cradle of Appalachian brandy lore:

"Golden apples make the best brandy. You take 'em and grind 'em in a little apple mill. Grind 'em just as fine as apple sauce. Put 'em in a 55-gallon wooden barrel and put a little water and a little sugar. How much sugar? Well, it's according to what grade brandy you're going to make. If you're going to make good brandy, you don't want to put but about 10 pounds in it. You don't have to put any sugar in it if you don't want to. The more sugar you put, of course, the more brandy you make, but it's worse brandy you make.

> *But, for what is Georiga famous?*
> *The products are many and fine,*
> *But there's one that outdoes the others,*
> *A jar of Georgia moonshine.*
> — *Anonymous*

"You could add ten pounds of sugar and about 10 gallons of water (add water only if you add sugar). By adding only 10 pounds of sugar, you wouldn't know the difference in it and pure apple brandy.

"The next day or two—after about 48 hours—it'll start working. Just bubbling like wine. You wait'll it sours down. In hot weather, it sours in about 10 days. The sides will fold in. The apples will fall in from the top.

"You have to stir it up good and taste it about three times with your tongue. It tastes as bitter as quinine. At that point, the pomace is about like apple sauce, and it's ready to still.

"You can run it in a copper pot or a steamer. As to a steamer, you have to have a big Hodge barrel—150 or 250-gallon Hodge barrel. Then get a thump barrel beside it, and a condenser. You can

Verner Fox of Dial, Ga., says brandy should be tempered with clear, cold water so that you can "get it down where it won't scorch your throat when you swaller it." Fox doesn't care for brandy except to smell it. "It smells like crabapple in the woods." But for drinking? "It's firey and too acidy for drinking." Verner remembers that his grandfather, George Fox, and his father operated a "government still" in the Stock Hill section. "A federal inspector would come ever so often and check it and take samples. They couldn't sell any at the still but they could give their friends a drink of it. They made some of the best rye whiskey in the world, and corn whiskey. They made it on copper stills, 60 to 75 gallons."

run it just as hot as you want. First time on a steamer, you put juice from the pomace in the thump keg. On the next run, put backings from the pot. Put about five gallons of pomace in it and five gallons of backin's.

"Out of 55 gallons of pomace, you'll get about 3 gallons of brandy. You'll get a gallon of brandy for each 10 pounds of sugar. You're better off with just 10 pounds of sugar, or none.

"It takes about 40 minutes to run off a still.

"It's 160/170 proof when it starts running. It's pure alkihol. So high it won't even bead. When it starts dying on down, it'll come to a bead. Finally, it'll flash off . . . about 90 proof. Then you catch your backin's. They're so weak, you don't use them. You put them back in the thump barrel and they come through again. Put in half backin's and half fresh pomace. Backin's just builds your alcohol up and starts you with a better kick. You take first shots—160 proof—right down to the last you catch—90 proof— and temper it with water. That brings it down to about 103. You don't run it again. You just blow it out on the ground and put a fresh batch in."

One last word, he emphasizes again that you'll get a whole lot more out of 'em if your apples are ground fine . . . almost like apple juice. "You grind core, seed and all . . . including worms."

"That's what helps them," his grandmother declared with a laugh. "And several yellow jackets."

Chapter
4

Corn Whiskies

"Makin' likker's hard work. I'd pick up two bushels of corn meal and go plum across the mountain, nearly two miles, carrying two bushels at a time on my shoulder. But I didn't care any more about that than nothin! . . ."

Corn Whiskies

Making corn whiskey, as anyone in the Appalachians will tell you, is an art, not merely boiling mash and running it through a still.

The secret is getting the right ingredients in those mash barrels, and giving them proper timing and sequence.

"It's like a woman making biscuits," says Short Stanton of Greene County, in East Tennessee. "If she don't know how to make them over thar in the mixing bowl, when she puts 'em in the pan, they ain't no count."

Whiskey distillers—somewhat akin to artists—are an individualistic bunch. Each has his own method and style. Some corn whiskey aficionados of the old school insist there is no way to make really good whiskey other than to use corn meal and corn malt exclusively with no sugar, no yeast (or "east" as many call it), no rye or barley malt. On the other hand, many modern practitioners insist that the addition of sugar and a bit of rye malt gives a run a lot more character and distinctive taste, and cuts down on its "corniness."

Without sugar or malt, incidentally, fermentation takes around 21 days, depending, of course, on the temperature. With the addition of sugar, the mashing-in time—from mash to distiller's beer—takes three to seven days, three in the summer time. By the

Hubert Howell checks out old still site in Cherokee County, Ga.

addition of yeast and/or malt, fermentation can be cut still another day.

Most moonshiners—old and young—have their own strong preferences about ingredients, having passed well beyond the early Kentucky mountain method of mixing in a "passel" of this and a "passel" of that.

There is, for example, some strong individual preference as to whether barley or rye malt (the sprouted grain, dried and ground) is a better additive to mash than corn malt. Most old folks like corn malt. The younger generation goes for barley.

Now to consider some of the corn whiskey recipes. Actually, although I had heard about spirits recipes being handed down from generation to generation, I didn't run into a single example, in my trips into the Appalachians, of a secret formula being inherited. Usually it has been a case of trial and experimentation through the years.

THE SIMMIE FREE SPECIAL

Simmie Free, my friend from Rabun County, Georgia, believes in making whiskey the old-fashioned way, but he was not a really "pure corn" advocate. His attitude was just about typical of most of the mountain moonshiners.

"I've made it out of corn meal, rye and nothin' else. But I got to where I could make it partly out of sugar and it was better likker than it was with pure corn.

"Well, now, listen, if you wanted ten gallons of likker out of two sixty-gallon barrels, two still fulls, put on a hundred pounds of sugar. You need about two or three bushels of corn meal. Heap of people say put a bushel and a half, but I like two and a half because it gives it that corn taste. Put in *plenty* of home-made malt. Just grind the fool out'n it and put it on. It'll really make likker.

"Now to make it the old-fashioned way, singlin' and doublin', you get your beer in the pot and cap it and get it to boiling, and you catch ye a gallon or two gallons of a singlin's to the singlin' run. Usually you'd have to run eight still fulls of singlin's to have enough for a doublin' run. Then you rinse your pot out good and clean, put those singlings in there and run it. When it comes out over hyar then it would be clear as a crystal and no drugs or nothin' about it, you know. You'd run it until it'd get to where it couldn't bead, when it 'broke at the worm', we called it. I could tell when it was 'breakin' at the worm', although I haven't used a worm in the last fifteen years. I use a double-wall condenser. But I could tell when it was breakin'. I could stand as fer as from here to that door yander and I could tell just when it would break. It quits runnin' nearly, the power and the strength stops . . . drops to a stream a little bittier than a match stem. I could take my finger and wet it that way and put it to my mouth and I could tell just the second I tasted it . . . didn't have the power.

"You take two half pint bottles of that high stuff, then put in one bottle full of nothin' but cold spring water. You stir it up together and it's pretty and clear. Then you got pretty, beaded likker. I mean *likker*. Good for anybody. Back when I made it, in 1938 when I moved to this place, I was gettin' anywhere from two to two and a half dollars to the gallon for it. I've been told by people if I could make it like I used to, singlin' and doublin', they'd be glad to pay me twenty-five dollars for ever gallon I could make. But a man can't do it today. Can't afford to.

"Now you never put in backin's to cut down your proof. Law, no, that'd make it taste bad. Don't put nothin' in to make it bead. I don't believe in that. You know, nowadays some people use beadin' oil and stuff. I don't believe in it. Beadin' oil won't kill you, but it ain't good for ye. I like it to have the power in there to make its own bead. And don't add too much water. If you do that, it wouldn't be likker. Be weak. That'd be selling water. A man do that, I don't believe in him. I believe in selling what is right."

Now for a rundown for a few recipes I picked up in my research travels for my earlier book, *Mountain Spirits*. First, a really old-fashioned pure corn version of doublin' whiskey—the kind affectionally called "double and twisted."

NORTH GEORGIA DOUBLE AND TWISTED

"Double and Twisted" whiskey, a favorite of old North Georgia distillers, is also called "Singlin' and Doublin'" in some localities. It is simply the distilling of whiskey twice (without the use of a "thumper" or "doubler" keg between the distilling pot and the condenser). The "twist" merely refers to the kinky twist the finished product takes when it pours from the worm. Here's how a doctrinaire double and twisted practitioner describes how he goes about making this powerful drink:

"You need a fifty-gallon still and eight fifty-gallon mash barrels. You will need to put three pecks of meal to each barrel and one peck of malt to each barrel. The more malt you use, the harder it will work, the quicker it will work off and the cornier it's a gonna taste. Malt makes it *mild*. Another thing makes it mild: Run that stuff just as cold as you can run it. Let the likker come out cold. If it runs hot it will be flat—even if it's pure corn.

> ". . . *Aye Goddd, drinking Cokee Coley*
> *and smoking cigarettes are going*
> *to be the ruination of this country.*
> *Now this corn cob pipe and a morning*
> *swig of corn whiskey—they are*
> *absolute needcessities . . . ."*
> —Old time Appalachian mountaineer Gid Moon
>   of Greenville, South Carolina

"Now for the steps:

"First, put water in your still up to the cape. Add your meal (three pecks) to the water before it gets too hot. Have one man pouring the meal in and one stirrin'. If you dump it in after the water's hot, you'll just have big clods in spite of everything and you'll have raw meal. After it starts boiling, keep it in the pot thirty minutes. Take it out then and put it in the mash barrel and add a gallon of raw meal in that. Let the barrel of mash set one day to the next. It'll go through a heating process. Be thick. A crust will develop on top and there'll be cracks in it like mud. You peel that crust off and throw it away. Then add water to it and add your malt to it then. Put a handful or two of raw rye meal. Helps the flavor and helps hold the bead. Stir it in until it's thoroughly mixed with the water. You need to make eight barrels like this.

"After the first run-off, throw away nearly all the pot tail. Just save enough pot tail to cook back about four bushels of meal for the next run. Mash that meal back in the scalding pot tail while it's hot too.

"On sweet mash run, the first one, you'll do well to get a gallon and a half to the bushel. On the next run, if you got real good corn, you'll make anywhere from two to three gallons, if you're a good distiller. Out of eight mash barrels you get enough to make two doublin' runs. Out of eight barrels, you'll get five to six gallons on the first run, and on the second run (if you use four bushels of meal) eight to twelve gallons. Out of those eight mash barrels, you'll end up with fifty gallons of singlins, and five or six gallons of doubling whiskey."

Oh, Georgia Booze is mighty fine booze,
The best yuh ever poured yuh,
But it burns the soles right off your shoes,
Cause hell's broke loose in Georgia.
      Stephen Vencent Benet (In Mountain Whipporwill)

HAMPER McBEE SPECIAL

Here in Hamper McBee's own inimitable style is his recipe for his favorite grain whiskey drink. Although Hamper is one of the greatest practitioners of the whiskey-making art, illicit style, he's not sold on pure corn at all. He prefers rye. Here's Hamper's recipe, along with his general comments:

"Most whiskey run now in this Cumberland Plateau country, they use yeast, which I never used in my life. Today, they just use rye bran, sugar, water and yeast. Have to use yeast. It ain't potent enough to work itself.

"If you use a steamer, rye and barley make the best whiskey, as far as I'm concerned. Back during World War II, when there was a shortage of sugar, lots of straight pure corn was made. Takes a long time. Have to sprout that old corn and grind it, a long process. I like rye—rye and barley.

"The first step, you put your rye meal and mix it up with boiling water. Mix it until it looks like cornbread batter ready to be baked. Let is set until it sours, then you break it up. You put your water and sugar and throw your whole grain rye (or barley) in and let it work off until it sours again.

"The first run is your sweet mash. You see, you don't throw that slop away. You keep using it over and over. You can use it for eight or ten runs. If you run one run a week don't throw it all away when you put it up. That keeps it from *all* being sweet mash. Sorta like sourdough. You catch all that slop and put it back in the mash box. You wait 'til it cools down. Can't put your malt in right away. If it's real hot, it'll kill the malt and it won't work off. If you can't hold your hand in the slop, you'd better not put up no rye meal, it'll kill the malt."

Hamper McBee

Rum by many is preferred
And brandy makes its boast.
The Dutch and English like their gin
And ale goes well with roast.
Requests for rye in Eastern States
Quite frequently are heard,
And the hill folk of the Southlands
Make corn a favorite word . . .

—Anonymous

THE LAUGHINGAL STEAMER EXPRESS

This recipe was given me by Hubert Howell, a retired moonshiner who used to do his makin' (in the late 1920's) around the Laughingal community in the lower reaches of Cherokee County, Georgia, near Lake Allatoona:

"We used yeast and barley malt. Used corn or rye meal. This is what we put into a thousand-gallon fermenter vat:

"Ten bags of sugar—or a thousand pounds; two bushels of corn meal or rye meal; some barley malt and yeast.

"You first put your water, meal, malt and yeast, and let it go to rollin'. After you broke it up and put the yeast in it, it'd be workin' in about six hours or less. Then you'd put the sugar in and then she would go to work . . . really begin to roll. After it quit workin' so hard, a big cap would come up on it. You know, about six or eight inches. When that cap went down and the top cleared, it was ready. Well, it'd be ready sometimes before that. Sometimes we wouldn't wait for it to fall. When it got bitter, too bitter to drink, it was ready to pump over to the steamer still for the boilin'."

GREENE COUNTY (TENNESSEE) CORNLICKER

This recipe comes from Short Stanton* in the valley east of Greeneville, Tennessee, in the shadow of the Great Smoky Mountains:

"Ain't but one way to make good straight corn likker. Your good steamer makes the purest likker there air. Take and scald your sweet mash. Pour water in up close to the cape. Pour ye two bushels of meal in thar. Stir it with your break stick. Stir it and let it start boilin'. Keep stirrin'. Let it boil about twenty minutes. Let that out. That's scalded. Have ye a gallon and half of good rye meal. Spread it all over the top of it. Cook it until fully done. Take your break stick—about so big around, about nine holes with pegs in it that long and sharp on each, and get ever speck of that meal all mashed up.

"Scald that today. Wait 'til day after tomorrow evenin'. Go back, take you a gallon and a half of good dried malt and pour ye water about that (six inches) close to the top. Get that malt all stirred up in that water, plum to the bottom of the barrel. Wait 'til the next mornin' and go back up. Take that break stick— you know it's all stewed up—and you can tear it up just as easy as you can with low meal. Then, let that go to work that day. Then

*Mr. Stanton has died since this interview was conducted.

Paul Robinson and Cecil Stockard look over old still site at Vinings, Ga., near Cumberland Mall north of Atlanta.

the next mornin', take and pour ye twenty-five pounds of sugar to the barrel, and let that work off.

"Run it out 'til you can take a proof bottle and hit it and when she all runs around it, little beads hang plum around it, half'n under and half up. Then you got about a hundred and five proof likker. Put that in a keg and let it stay three weeks. Go to the keg about twice a day and shake her real good. Take the stopper out. In three weeks, it'll be cherry red. That's some of the *best* likker that you've ever stuck in your mouth. She'll char more that way in three weeks than hit will settin' right there perfectly still in six months. That's kerrect."

A friend from Greeneville—Colonel L.B. Britton—who took me out to visit Short, confirmed that Stanton "never did make any mean likker."

Stanton himself affirmed it. "Ask any man in Greene County, North Carolina or wherever they drunk any of my likker. It was always good. I forget now which one of these revenue officers told it right here in federal court. Said they could eat right off the top of my still furnace."

"Back in thirty-three, we couldn't get money
in any other way. Everybody nearly back then was in
whiskey. Anybody that you seed riding in a car
had something to do with whiskey, now, some way
a'nother . . . either bootlegged, hauled it or made it."
—*Hubert Howell of Cartersville,*
Ga., ex-moonshiner.

KENNESAW MOUNTAIN DRINKIN' LIKKER

This recipe comes from an ex-moonshiner who lives near Big Shanty in sight of Kennesaw Mountain, Georgia. Here are his comments:

"If I was going to make some likker for me to drink myself, I'd take a couple of bushels of corn meal, cook it, put it in with about a hundred pounds of sugar and cap it with malt. Purpose of the cap is to keep the alcohol and heat in. I wouldn't use any east (sic). Let it work off by itself in wooden vat or barrels. Take anywhere from five to ten days in warm weather. I'd run it through the thumper and get ten or twelve gallons out of it."

HUBERT HOWELL, an ex-moonshiner who did most of his illicit whiskey-making during the National Prohibition days in the late 20's and early 30's, is a steamer still whiskey advocate. "It's the best they are," he says. "Steamer still whiskey is never burned. Ain't got no burnt taste. Now, on these copper pots, you can't help but scorch the whiskey ever once in a while. Don't make no difference how careful you are, because you've got to empty that mash in that hot pot, you see, and before you can fill it up, it's going to stick and scorch."

BREVARD, NORTH CAROLINA SPECIAL

This one was given to me by an old timer near Brevard, North Carolina. He first offered, at my request, a pure grain recipe, but was quick to add his preference for a grain-sugar likker. Here is his pure grain version:

"Get four bushels of corn meal, and mash it in a barrel of water. Add one bushel of rye meal and one bushel of ground up sprouted corn (malt). Let it all work off and pour in the pot and distill."

But he likes this one better, which he calls "Sour Mash Sugar Likker": "Take a hundred pounds of sugar, add a bushel of rye and slop from the last run. Let ferment and distill. Makes twelve gallons. I like this sugar likker a lot better than corn. Corn's too fiery!"

CUMBERLAND CORN LICKER (BLACK POT STYLE)

Here's a recipe for "Black Pot Drinkin' Licker" as concocted by a moonshiner on the Cumberland Plateau near Tracy City, Tennessee:

"Well, to start off, you charge your mash boxes with meal and sugar. Fifty pounds of sugar and one peck of meal. That's five gallon of whiskey. Put it in a sixty-gallon barrel. You cook that meal in there (with steam) and you don't touch it no more until the next mornin'. Then you break that all up, put warm water in it. Put it up right close to the top, you see. She's done soured, then put you in ten pounds of sugar 'n' when it starts workin' good, go back and put all your sugar in, see. You got to break that meal up, you see, when it goes to crackin' and poppin', that's when you break it."

The same moonshiner had another recipe which was about the same, except for the addition of corn malt. Here's how it goes:

"You make a mash box out of poplar. You add the water to the meal and sugar. Just put enough water in it so it will be pretty thin . . . soupy. You kinda cook that in with live steam. To make you a malt, take corn and sprout it. Put your (shelled) corn in a tow sack and bury it in a sawdust pile. When the sprout gets up on it about two inches long, take that out and grind it in a sausage mill. Add that to your mash. That's your corn malt and that will start your beer to workin'. It will foam up and make a big foamy cap. When that cap goes down, just as that quits, your beer has the most alcohol content, you run it. At that point, you fire up your cooker."

Now for a really old-fashioned
pre-Civil War corn whiskey recipe from Kentucky:
1823 KENTUCKY SWEET MASH

This recipe appeared in the *Kentucky Gazette* of Lexington, Kentucky, on November 27, 1823, quoting a pamplet, "A Receipt for distilling by a process called the sweet mash, by which an average of two gallons of excellent spirit has been made by a noted distiller in the neighborhood of Lexington." Here is the complete recipe:

"Pour twelve gallons of boiling water into an hundred gallon tub, add one handful of hops, then half a bushel of corn-meal, stir the contents well, again pour in twelve gallons of boiling water and half bushel of meal, repeating the stirring to prevent the meal

"There's nothing that will
life you up like a dram of
corn liquor in the morning."
—From old time Kentucky mountain ballad

from collecting into lumps. Then pour in twelve gallons more of water and another half bushel of meal, and stir again; let it stand until so cool the distiller can bear his hand four inches within the surface of the mash, without more pain than a slight stinging sensation at the ends of his fingers.

"Then put in a half a gallon of malt and four gallons of rye or wheat meal, after which, stir the vessel about half-way, to the bottom, so as to wet the meal, and let stand ten minutes; then stir down to the bottom, and repeat the stirring every ten minutes until the liquor shall be about milk-warm, or until you can insert your hand into it nine inches without pain. Fill up the tub within four or five inches of the top with cold or cool water, then add half a gallon of yest (sic), and if the weather be very cold, the tub may be covered over with a mat for one night. The tub is then suffered to stand until the bubbles cease to rise, then it will be ready for distillation; and after being well stirred up, the beer should be poured into the still for distillation."

SOUTHWEST VIRGINIA STRAIGHT CORN

Down in the southwest tip of Virginia, old timers still make corn whiskey in the old-fashioned way. Here is how John S., now deceased, described his recipe as recorded by Earl Palmer: "The way I make my whiskey, I use a bushel of fine ground corn meal in the barrel (52 gallons), which I scald for two hours until it settles like a batch of cornbread. I let it set for twenty minutes, then beat it down about four inches the first time. Wait another twenty minutes then beat it down again, then blend well with hot water.

"Let the mash cool until you can hold your arm in it, than add one gallon of corn malt which I make from sprouted corn. I let my mash work for eight or ten days atop this mountain, then I stir my mash real good and start my still up over a slow fire to keep my whiskey from scorching.

"I let my likker run off till it draps the head, then I let about a quart of backins run off to proof my first shots down with. The yield is a gallon and pint of pure corn whiskey."

As photographer/writer Palmer says, "This very old-time way produced drinkin' likker fit for a king . . . likker a feller could drink all day long without getting a hangover."

The late "Peg" Fields had a unique method for aging whiskey. "I can go right over there and cut me down a white oak, or hickory, strip me out some strips about five inches long and just cover that heater (on top), burn 'em just as black as the ace of spades. Turn 'em over, but let 'em catch a-faar. I'd drop about three or four of them sticks in that jug right there if it was full of brandy or whiskey. It'll turn that whiskey just as perfect as one of them (charred) barrels will. In a week or two's time, go back and look at it. Start turning red. You shake that up and keep shaking it. Next thing you know, it's just as pretty as any charted (charred barrel) whiskey you've ever seen."

Lanky ex-corn whiskey distiller Theodore King—who has manned the moonshine still exhibit at the Georgia Mountain Fair at Hiawassee, Georgia for a number of years—shows how to properly drink moonshine from a jug or gallon jar. You merely cradle the jug in the crook of the arm and raise it ever so slightly. "It takes a little doing," says Thee. "There's an art to it, just like in cooking up a batch of corn whiskey."

GREAT SMOKY MOUNTAIN CORNLICKER

Here is a recipe for corn liquor that is posted next to an old copper pot still on display in the Pioneer Museum at the Oconaluftee Visitor Center, Great Smoky Mountains National Park near Gatlinburg, Tennessee:

- 1 80-gallon still
- 1 60-gallon barrel
- 4 bushels of corn, not too fine
- ½ bushel of rye, ground coarse
- ½ bushel sprouted corn, dried and ground malt

Mix together, scald and pat like dough. Let stand twenty-four hours. Then put in barrel and fill with water. Let it work eight-ten days or until cap falls off. Makes two gallons to the bushel.

KENTUCKY MOUNTAIN CORN

This recipe comes from an old-time moonshiner in the Cumberland Plateau country just north of the Cumberland Gap made famous by Daniel Boone:

"Pour twenty-five pounds of coarsely ground corn meal in a

Mrs. Noah Chitwood (L) of Habersham County was a wee lass (around 3 years old) when photo below was made in the late 1800s at the old Maxwell Corn Whiskey Distillery, a registered "Government Distillery" near Baldwin, Ga. It was typical of the registered distilleries in operation across the South following the Civil War. In the old photo, the man at the left with hammer in hand, is the Government "gauger," (inspector) Reuben Nunnally. He made certain the spirits were of the proper strength and poof and on his visits checked the distillery's books and collected the excise taxes. He was posing as if he were stamping the barrel's content and strength with steel dies.

Docie (Mrs. Noah) Chitwood, one of the little girls in the photo, was visiting the distillery with her mother in background left. Stirring mash in vat in foreground was Oscar Master, who had migrated from Scotland. L-R in background: Mr. and Mrs. Allen Stewart, Docie's uncle and aunt. Note wagon in left background. The Negro driver had a fresh load of whiskey which was to be put on the train in Baldwin, bound for Atlanta.

mash barrel. Add scalding hot water. When the mixture cools add a peck of corn malt and fifty pounds of white sugar and fill the barrel with water. Stir well and let it stand and ferment for six days, or until the cap falls. whichever is fastest. When fully fermented, put it in a pot and distill."

HOG LIKKER

"Hog Likker" is the kind you make in a groundhog still. In the groundhog still, the mash fermentation and distilling is done in the same container. Here is how a still operator from Forsyth

Hamper McBee looks over old still site in Cumberland Plateau, Tennesee.

County, Georgia described the making of a batch of "hog likker."

"For a five-hundred gallon still, you first have to put in a hundred pounds of malt sprouts and put a pound of sugar to each gallon of water—five hundred pounds. Then you cap it off with wheat bran. When it ferments, you boil it and it'll make, in that five-hundred gallon still, about seventy-five gallons of likker. That's *hog likker*. You don't 'slop it out.' After a run you just leave it in there. When you get through cooking, you still have four-hundred gallons of water in there. You just have to add on some water and the same amount of sugar—five hundred pounds— and fifty pounds of malt."

*　　*　　*

A reminder: These so-called "recipes" have been collected for their humor value but take heed, don't try to distill a batch yourself. You could get in big trouble. To reiterate, it is strictly against federal law to distill alcohol without a federally-registered, tax paid distillery. And the ATF doesn't lightly hand out permits for distilling. You can't get one unless there is a serious commercial intent and an adequate facility.

The federal regulations do allow a head of a household to ferment wine (up to two hundred gallons a year) or make cider in his own home. To do this, however, you should get a permit from the Bureau of Alcohol, Tobacco and Firearms. To get the address of your local ATF regional office, write to the ATF national headquarters in Washington.

Chapter 5

Moonshiners and Trippers

Moonshining has been one of the constant truths about the South for all these years, right up there with segregation and hard shell religion.

— Paul Hemphill

Moonshiners
and
Trippers

JUNIOR SAMPLES, the "Hee Haw" tv comedian who lives at Cumming, Georgia has had plenty of experience in the moonshine game all the way from distilling to tripping the mountain spirits into Atlanta. Junior says, "If you make good moonshine likker, you've got to have corn, although corn doesn't pay off as far as 'selling likker' is concerned. I've used a lot of wheat bran and sugar, which during the war was twenty-five dollars a sack on the black market. Wheat bran will give your must as much fire in your likker and you can get drunk on it three times down. Also bran builds up the volume. Now if you put corn meal in it, of you get drunk one time, you're damn drunk. I ain't drunk any moonshine in several years. All the moonshine I get, I give it to my best friends."

FRED GOSWICK JR., one-time moonshine tripper from Dawson County into Atlanta, drove many a 1940 Ford "opera coupe" such as this one. He delivered many loads to the parking lot of Atlanta's old Southern Railway "Terminal Station," to a spot near the "Fabulous Fox" theater on Peachtree street, and one time deposited 240 half-gallon fruit jars (20 cases) of a white whiskey to a garage almost in the shadow of Georgia's gold-domed State Capitol building.

"We used to pull off the expressway on North Avenue and park there near the Varsity restaurant. One time my cousin came off there with a load and the police pulled him over. He jumped out and started running and the police chased him. A few minutes later, my brother drove up and saw what had happened, so he jumped into the cousin's car and took it to a stash garage.

When the police caught my cousin and brought him back to North Avenue, he really raised hell because they had let his car get stolen. They turned him loose after 72 hours because they didn't have any evidence." One time a policeman pulled Goswick over in Atlanta and asked for his driver's license.

"Dawson County, eh?" The policeman smiled. "What do you do?"

"I farm," Goswick replied.

"Farm, hell," the officer replied. "I never saw a Dawson County boy yet that didn't 'farm'. I know you boys are running moonshine down here, but please keep your cars off the streets and out of our no-parking zones."

Earl Palmer

ARTHUR YOUNG, 76, who lives near the headwaters of the Tallulah River in Rabun County, Georgia, remembers that making whiskey in the mountains near Clingman's Dome, North Carolina in his youth was hard work. "I've heard it said back in them days, 'That man ought to be out workin' instead of makin' likker. He ain't doin' nothing, just taking it easy.' The fact was, the moonshiners were the ones who were *really* working. We carried meal in on our backs. Take it on wagon or horseback as far as you could, then you'd put it on your shoulders. A bushel of meal would weigh 62 pounds. Back then I was young enough to take it. I was stout. At 18, I didn't know how stout I was. We brought the liquor out in five and ten-gallon kegs (weighing 40 and 80 pounds each)." Young is pictured at the moonshine still exhibit at the Georgia Mountain Fair.

Young also is an accomplished fiddler and owns a violin that is a hundred years old. "I had an Antonio Stradivarius fiddle burn up in my house near here. Made in 1700. My greater grandfather brought it from England. But I enjoy playing the one I got now. I know a lot of tunes that have never been put down to record."

"Making moonshine was hard work all right,
but if you stayed about half drunk, you didn't care."
—Dawsonville, Georgia,
ex-moonshiner

"You're afraid when you first get into it,
but it ain't long before you can lay down by one
of 'em stills and go to sleep."
—Retired moonshiner from
Cherokee County, Georgia

THE "MALTING IN" STAGE. A moonshiner pours in a mixture of yeast and warm water to mash barrels to "kick it off." Several days later, the mash has become "still beer," with an alcoholic content of about 10 per cent and is "just right to run." The barrels pictured here are 150-gallon size and will yield about 10 to 13 gallons of whiskey each, depending on how well the mash works off. A rule of thumb has it that a bushel of meal and 100 pounds of sugar will yield 10 gallons of whiskey on the first (sweet mash) run and much more on the subsequent "slopping back" (sour mash) distillations.

AMOS OWENS was one of the most famous of the defiant moonshiners who emerged in the South following the Civil War. Owner of Cherry Mountain in Rutherford County, North Carolina, Amos—like his compatriots across the South—came home to find that not only had the Confederates lost the War, but that they had lost the right to distill corn whiskey and apple brandy without government interference and taxation. Thus Uncle Amos in the late 1800's had numerous run-ins with "the Federal," the hated revenooers. Owens, a great corn whiskey chef, was famous for his corn whiskey-based "Cherry Bounce." First of all, he grew giant black heart cherries on his mountain and had his daughters crush them with their bare feet in a giant vat. Then he mixed the resulting cherry juice with sourwood honey and a generous portion of his famous corn whiskey. Every June, he staged a big festival atop Cherry Mountain and served his guests a feast, plied them with Cherry Bounce and offered numerous games of entertainment, including gander-pulling.

Here is a more modern recipe for Cherry Bounce, as compiled by the Junior Service League of Johnson City, Tennessee, in their book of recipes, *Smoky Mountain Magic*: "To one gallon of white spirits put two quarts of water and five or six quarts of white cherries. Wash cherries and put in jug with alcohol. Corn cob stopper in jug. Let stand for three months. Drain off liquor and strain well. Make a thick syrup with one and one-half pounds white sugar and water and boil until ropy. Add the syrup to liquor to taste."

The late *PEG FIELDS* of Jasper, Ga., remembered making corn whiskey in the old fashioned way that was fit for a king. "If I had some now, I could get $25 or $30 a gallon, just like that (snapping his finger.). It'd sell, too. You could drink it, wouldn't need no water with it, just as mild as it could be. It was up there close to a hundred proof. Had a bead on it about as big as the end of your finger. You could shake that up and that bead'd just stand up there all around. You could just turn it up, drink it just about like drinking water. After a little, it'd get you too. After a while, if you drink enough of it, it'd make you drunk. We got a big price for it back then, $2 a gallon for sugar whiskey and three dollars for pure corn. Now it'd bring $25 or $30 a gallon. I always kept a gallon of that sweet mash whiskey. I was farmin'. Fifteen acres I tended. I took a gallon across the creek in bottoms and dug me a hole. This old gray dirt. It was shady in there. Glass jug. Just as clear. I drunk that down. It was about half full. I'd go up for my jug ever so often. It was so clear I couldn't tell if it was full or empty, just as clear as it could be. They've got a legal still in Albany (Georgia). I'd pay them a thousand dollars to let me make a hundred gallons if they'd let me make it and if they'd let me set it up." (Mr. Fields died in 1977)

HAMPER McBEE looks over old still site on the side of the mountain near St. Mary's, Tennessee. A stream of limestone water runs from inside the cave to a sink hole near the front of the cave. Hamper remembered trying to ferment mash at such a site in the cold of winter. "One time we were under a bluff like this. It was down to zero and the branch was frozen solid, but those boxes of mash were 'working' . . . There wasn't a bit of ice in it. It was workin', just boilin'. We broke the ice off the side of the bluff and filled the flake stand full of ice. Big sheets of ice as big as this wall. Like to froze our hands off. We'd taken an axe and break it. Seeming like a ton of ice would fall. We fired up that still. Lord, it like to worked us to death. It mailed out pretty quick. We run thirty gallons from three-hundred pounds of sugar to the box."

"This is black pot country," says Hamper. "You put an old pot in the ground and you put your mash and everything in the pot and build your fire around it and that's what you call a duck nest. You just build your furnace around your pot. You can make more money with a black pot outfit because sometimes you can get fourteeen, fifteen gallons out of a batch on a pot when you might get ten gallons out of an average run on a steam outfit."

THUNDER ROAD PROTOTYPE—Stock car racing got its start in the Southern Appalachians. The original "good old boy" whose career meshed whiskey hauling with race driving was Lloyd Seay of Dawsonville. Seay was famous for his ability to outwit lawmen on whiskey runs into Atlanta and he was equally successful as a driver on the dirt Lakewood Speedway in Atlanta. Seay won the National Stock Car Racing Championship Sept. 1, 1941, at Lakewood but was killed by a cousin the following day near Dawsonville in an argument about sugar. Friends and family had his tombstone adorned with a carving of his 1939 Ford coupe, and attached his photo to the window.

Whiskey "run"   Earl Palmer

Chapter 6

Building a Copper Pot Still

Mountain people are action seekers. They live episodically and they live for adventure. Moonshining for some of them is the ultimate adventure.

— John Gordon, in The Georgia Review.

Building a
Copper Pot Still
The Thee King Way

Theodore J. King looks a lot like Abraham Lincoln. Especially when he lets his beard get bushy and when he unlimbers his bony, six-foot frame. The profile is striking. People who attend the Georgia Mountain Fair in August in Hiawassee, Georgia, like to snap pictures of Theodore in front of his 50-gallon copper rig. He'll even hoist up one of those stone jugs for the touristers with cameras--you know, just like Snuffy Smith: One handed, with the jug cradled snugly on his shoulder and the juice gurgling merrily into his gullet.

Thee King—"old doc" as he likes to call himself—was "borned into whiskey" in 1918 in the Gum Log Mountain district of Towns County, way up in North Georgia's Appalachian Mountains next to the North Carolina line. He inherited his ability to make whiskey and to build stills. His father Tom King, a half Cherokee

Indian, and his Grandfather King, a full-blood Cherokee, were past masters in the stilling and still-making art. "For that was the only way we had of making an honest dollar when we were growing up and the people in back of me."

Thus when he was six years old, Thee was crawling down into 35-gallon pots, holding the swage while his daddy and granddaddy put in the rivets. Two years later, in 1926, eight-year-old Thee King helped build his first still. "It was in the fall of the year," King remembered. "Our still-making grounds were down in the Winchester Cove in Gum Log Mountain. We had twin poplar stumps . . . one tree was seven and a half foot through, and the other seven. They were cut down by Frank Paine in 1933. Yeah, that was our old still-making grounds. Me and my younger brother built that first still. Of course, my dad and Uncle Joe and Jim Keats helped us on it. But I cut it out myself. I done everything but when we went to puttin' it together, my daddy come along and 'stepped the bottom' fer me (with a big compass)."

Still making at Gum Log got to be a big industry in 1928. "That's when Hoover got in. It was damn rough, and people were calling for our stills from all over. We averaged two and sometimes three stills a week. We made 'em for *ever*'body all the way from Tennessee, South Carolina, plum on down below Atlanter, for people in Valdosta, several in Ohio and Virginia."

The Gum Log still makers charged $1 a gallon to make stills, with the buyer furnishing all of the copper and rivets. Sizes ranged from 135 down to 80 and 85 and down to 25 gallons. The favorite was 35 gallons capacity, although in later years the 50-gallon unit predominated.

So for 12 years—from 1928 until Thee went into the CCC Camp in 1940—he was heavily engaged in still-making. He figures more than 800 stills were built during this period, at an average of six stills a month. And he built, or helped build, all of them.

So Thee King knows how to build stills. Today, in semi-retirement due to disability brought on by tuberculosis that caused him to lose one lung, King continues to build stills. Only today, he makes one and two-gallon model stills for the tourist trade.

Here, step by step, is how Thee King builds a two-gallon copper pot still, mostly in his own words:

Perhaps first of all there should be some explanation of terms, since they will be used frequently in this chapter. The main components are: Pot; Cape; Collar; Cap; Cap Arm; Thump Keg; Long Thump Post; Short Thump Post; Condenser; Slop Arm

In addition, there are special vapor line connections which are required to get the spirit vapors from the cooking pot across to the condenser.

Now that we have an understanding of the components, here is Thee's list of materials required:

3' x 4' sheet of 36 gauge copper. This is actually a "half sheet" since copper comes in 4 x 8 foot sheets. This should be soft, pliable copper, and should be 16-ounce copper, meaning it weighs a pound for every square foot.

A half sheet will cost you roughly $25, although the price of copper is volatile. Earlier in 1975, this same half-sheet cost $32.

Solder. Get acid core, not rosin type. It comes in rolls in a green box.

Copper rivets. These must be quarter-inch, 12 gauge, with burrs.

2-gallon wooden keg. This is the "thump keg." One inch holes must be bored on each side of the top of this, one for the insertion of the "thump post" and the other for insertion of the "headache piece." A ½-inch hole should be bored in the side of the bottom to draw the "feints" out, after a run.

Square wooden box. This is the "flake stand," to hold the condensing unit. This should be approximately 8 inches by 8 inches by 8 inches in size.

TOOLS: Here are the tools needed to build this still:
Sheet metal shears ("Rights" and "lefts").
Tin snips.
Large construction compass.
Rivet set (punch, swage and ice pick).
Pliers (Wire pliers to do crimping).
Hammer (16-02 ball peen hammer preferred). Claw hammer okay.

Stump (or section) of tree (to be used for punching holes into copper sheet).

2" x 2" piece of iron or steel (two or three feet long). (This is for riveting work).

2 steel pipes (plain metal water pipes. One should be 1½ inches in diameter, the other about ¾ or 5/8 inches).

Ruler

Good straight edge, possibly a yard-stick, if it is good and straight.

Pencil.

1
These are the tools Thee King uses to build a 2-gallon copper still.

2

Thee cuts 7-inch strip of copper sheeting, then cuts the four identical pieces for the pot.

THE PATTERN

There is plenty of copper in a 3 x 4 half sheet to build this unit, but not enough to allow waste.

The first step is to take the pattern and cut out the parts. Let's begin with the pot:

POT:

This requires four exact size pieces. All of these pieces will be seven inches deep. So first of all, take your ruler and measure off seven inches on each edge of the three-foot wide sheet of copper. Take your straight edge and mark it off across. Now it is ready to be cut out with your tin snips.

You have now a piece of copper three feet wide and seven inches deep For the first piece, measure seven inches wide, which will give you a piece seven inches square. Cut it out. Now take your ruler and on top side measure in three quarters of an inch on each side. Take your straight edge or ruler and mark off a line

3

These four pieces will be used to form bottom of the pot.

from this three/quarters indentation on the top down to the edge on the bottom. On both sides. Now cut out. This is your pattern for the four pieces for the pot. Use this first piece as the pattern for your other three pieces. Cut out precisely.

Next you must punch the holes out for riveting the four pieces together. From the bottom of each piece, measure up a half inch and with your straight edge, make a pencil mark across from one side to the other. Now, on each side, measure in a quarter of an inch. Make a mark at the bottom and another at the top. Take your compass and mark a line from top to bottom. Do the same on the other side. Where the lines intersect on the bottom is where your first rivets go. Now take your compass and set it for one inch between points. Beginning with the bottom rivet point, take your compass and mark off the other rivet points. You will have seven rivet points on each side. Mark off these exact rivet points on each of the other three pieces.

Now get out your punch and hammer and your wooden stump. Take the point of the punch and place it exactly on the point made by your compass. Give it a good lick or two with the hammer. It should punch out cleanly. If you have trouble later in inserting a rivet, use an ice pick to ream it out a bit.

RIVETING THE POT

You should now have in hand four identical pieces of copper, each of which has 14 holes punched out, seven on each side. Now you are reday to begin riveting. Get out your heavy piece of 2 x 2 iron to use as your riveting base to lay the copper on. Place this iron bar from the ground up to your stump. Now take piece one of your copper on the right and lap its left edge of the top of the right edge of piece two. Take one of your rivets and from underneath, fit it into piece two, then through its corresponding hole in piece one. On top, put the burr (washer) over the rivet. Smash it down a bit with your hammer, just enough to hold it in place. Now do the same thing with the rivet on the other end of these pieces. Next, take your swage and hammer and flatten out this rivet, using your piece of iron underneath as your solid base. Follow through with all four pieces.

Now you come to the point of connecting piece four with piece one. Here you must "roll" these four connected pieces into a round pot. You do this (see photo), by grasping piece one firmly with both hands and, inch-by-inch, roll the copper until it is bent into a roll. Go on to pieces two, three and four. If it is not rolled

4
Holes are punched, seven to a side, to make a seam.

5

Rivets are placed through the two pieces. Swage and hammer are used to accomplish a good connection.

enough to make the connection, go back and gently continue this rolling from the beginning until you achieve it. Then rivet pieces one and four together.

THE CAPE

Now you should have a completely riveted pot. Set it aside temporarily and get to work on the cape, the upper part of the pot. Here you follow the same procedure as on the pot. First, measure off a four inch strip of copper sheeting and cut it out. Now mark off eight-inch wide section. On these pieces, you have a 2¼-inch offset at the top of each piece, so on your first piece, your pattern, mark off this 2¼-inch offset to the inside of each side, right and left, at the top. Now take your pencil and mark this pattern from top to bottom. Now cut out the piece with tin snips. Cut carefully and accurately. You now have the pattern for the four pieces for your cape. Cut them out. Next you mark off the holes for the rivets, just as on your pot. Each piece will have six rivet holes, three on each side. First mark off across the bottom a straight line one-half inch from the bottom edge. Now pencil in a line on the inside of each side. This will be one quarter of an inch

6
"Rolling" the copper creates a round form.

7
King rivets the
pot, using iron
bar underneath.

from the edge. Now take your pencil and line off this line from top to bottom. Again, where your pencil lines intersect at the bottom will be your rivet points. Now take your compass, set it at one inch and mark off the rivet points, going from bottom to top. Follow through the same as on the pot. First punch out the holes, put in the rivets and burrs, and lock them in with the swage and hammer. Roll the four pieces and attach them, just as on the pot.

Now comes a somewhat tedious but a very crucial part of the still-making process. You will notice that the top and bottom of this cape are not round. You have pieces sticking out. You must use your tin snips now to cut off these jagged pieces. First, just

8
Cutting four pieces for the cape.

clip off the pieces sticking out. Next, go around the bottom and top with your shears, rounding it off. Before you make the final cut on the top of the pot and the bottom of your cape, place the two parts together to see if they are going to have a fairly good fit.

9
Rivet holes are punched.

10
Four pieces for the cape, readying for riveting.

11
King admires his handiwork.

BOTTOM OF THE POT

The next step is that of putting the bottom on the pot.

First, take a piece of remaining copper and place the pot down over it. Take your pencil or a nail and mark down an outline of the bottom of the pot onto the sheet. Put aside the pot. Now measure the diameter of this circle. Divide this number by two. Set your compass to this figure and locate the exact center of this circle. Use the compass to scribe the exact mark for the bottom

12
Tin snips are used to trim around bottom and top of cape to round them out.

13
Fitting cape to pot to check for good fit.

sheet. Now, you need to reset your compass an additional one-eighth of an inch. Now circumscribe this mark, outside the original mark. This outer ring is the one you must cut with your snips. Now comes a tedious job. Take your pliers and slowly and deliberately bend upward a one-eighth of an inch lip. Eventually, you want this lip to be at a 90-degree angle (to allow the pot to be set down into it snugly). However, you start with your pliers, one bite at a time, and you bend it up ever so slightly. The second time around, you can bend it further. By the third or fourth time round, you can get it to the desired right angle.

ANOTHER METAL BENDING EXERCISE

Now you have one more metal bending exercise: The top of the pot. You need to bend it "in" at the top—again like a pie crust—but it doesn't have to be 90 degrees. Only about 45 degrees. This is to effect a snug fit of the pot and the cape. In other words, the cape must fit down into the pot for about an eighth of an inch. This eighth of an inch at the top of the pot must be bent in to effect a snug fit. So again, you take your pliers in hand. Remember, this is *only one-eighth of an inch.* So gently bend down only the very edge. Slowly make your way around the entire pot. It may take one or two more rounds.

14
Marking bottom of pot, using pot as pattern.

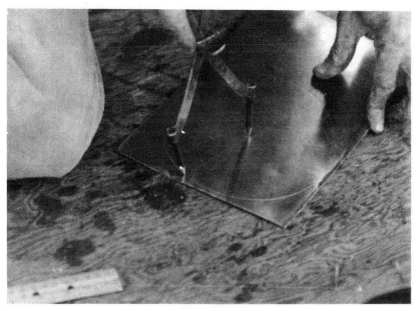

15
Compass is used to scribe exact pattern to cut.

16
Trimming top of pot.

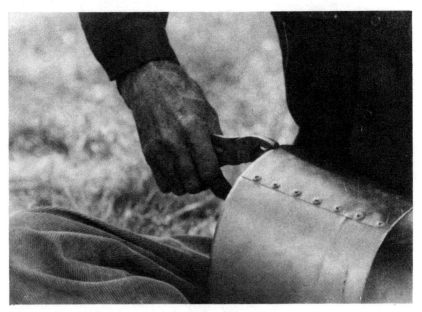

17
Top of pot must be bent in with pliers to 45 degree angle.

THE COLLAR

Put aside the pot and cape and leave them until you need to start soldering. Your next job is building the collar to fit into the top of the pot. This collar will enable you to fit your still cap down into the still snugly, and pull it back out quickly and easily.

You can cut your cap and collar from the same piece of copper. It should be 13½ inches long and four inches wide. Mark this off with your yard stick or straight edge and cut it out. Your collar should be one-inch wide and your cap three inches wide. So mark off the one-inch wide collar, and cut it out. Now, you must cut one-quarter of an inch off of the end of the collar. You'll understand the reason for this later. But the piece for the collar should be one inch wide and 13¼ inches long. Now, across the length of this piece of collar make a nail mark one-eighth of an inch deep, from one end of the collar to the other. This is for your guidance in bending over the metal (with the pliers and hammer) to give it a "tin lock" double thickness, an additional strength of reinforcement. But before you start this metal-bending, you need to make two more marks. At each end, make a straight line top

18
The collar is attached with one rivet.

19
Checking the collar and top of cape.

to bottom, one-quarter of an inch from each edge. Now take your compass and, with it set on one-half an inch, place a point where the one-half intersects with the penciled mark. On both ends. This is your rivet mark. In other words, after you have doubled down the one-eighth inch at the top, and after you have gently "rolled" the collar around to a perfectly round circle, you will put it together with one rivet! Punch out the rivet hole as in the earlier steps.

Now, start bending the top of the collar down. Eventually, this bend should be "out"—on the outside of the rounded collar. This bending is going to have to be done so that it is completely doubled back and hammered down, or tin-locked. So the word at this point is—patience! Go slowly and deliberately. You may not want to accomplish it all at one sitting. But gradually, with your pliers, go down this sheet—one bite at a time, until you have reached the end. Then go back and start over. When you get it bent over sufficiently, you can use your hammer to help out.

Once the piece bending has been completed, you must now start "rolling" the collar into a circle. You "roll" it the same way you did the pot and the cape—with your hands at first. After you have got it going, you can hammer it from the inside to help get it into a perfect circle. Now lap it over your iron rod and rivet it. Put it aside.

THE CAP

You already have the piece cut out for the cap. It is 13½ inches long and three inches wide. Now, make a nail mark all the way across the top of this piece, one-eighth of an inch down on the right end. Now do the same for the left. Now use your straight edge and mark it off. This is for bending it down a bit.

Next, you mark the spots for the two rivets required to put the cap together. On the right end, a quarter of an inch from the end, place a mark from top to bottom. Do the same for the left end, top to bottom. Now take your compass and place a rivet mark one inch from the bottom, on the pencil mark. Now go up another inch and place the second rivet mark. Do the same on the left end. Punch out the four rivet holes.

Next, you "round" this cap by rolling it first with your hands. Keep rolling it until it is almost in a circle. Now, before you rivet it take your pliers and bend in—to a 90-degree angle—the one-eighth inch strip across the top of your cap. This may require two rounds. This 90-degree down-bend is needed to have a base for the soldering of the dome. Here again, patience is the word. It's tiresome, but don't despair. Now rivet your cap with the two rivets.

20
Cap is fabricated with two rivets.

THE CAP TOP

This one takes a bit of doing but it will be a lot of fun. Thee calls this job "plumbing" the cap top. Actually, you've got to make a dome to fit over the top of your cap. The way you do it is to take a hammer and actually hand stamp the metal into a dome.

First of all, take your completed cap shell and place it down on your remaining copper sheet. Use your pencil to outline the circle of the cap. Now cut it out with your tin snips.

Now comes the fun part. Take the round cap top and place it on the ground, preferably soft dirt. Take your hammer and hit it hard, right in the center. Now start hammering out a circle from the center, round and round. Cock the hammer at an angle so you can ' stretch" the copper. Once you have hammered your way in circles to the outer edge, reverse your hammering and hammer your way back, round and round, to the center. Give a few more solid strikes down in the center—straight down. Make your way back to the outer edge again. By this time, your top should be shaping up nicely as a dome. Eyeball it carefully. It may need a few licks here and there to give it uniformity. Put it aside until you get to the soldering stage.

21
Checking collar/cap fit.

22
King cuts cap top, a 4½-inch diameter circle.

THE CONDENSER

The really old-fashioned copper pot stills had copper coil condensers, but the most popular condenser since 1900—one that was called just that, "condenser"—was a double-walled unit that is not too difficult to build. The major hurdles are metal-bending and soldering.

You have two basic condenser pieces, the outside shell and the inside shell. Both measure six inches deep. The outside shell measures nine inches wide, while the inside shell measures eight inches wide. Mark these off and cut them out. On the inner shell, mark off a line across the top and bottom one-fourth inch in from top and the same for the bottom.

Both of these are rolled and soldered, not riveted. In order to roll them, put them around the big pipe, and roll them with your hands, a half inch at a time. Take the right side (end) and lap it one-quarter inch over the end of the left side. Do the same for both the inner shell and outer shell. They are ready for soldering. But we will await the soldering until we get to the section on soldering, coming next. However, you should go ahead and bend the top and the bottom of the inner shell. Using the line marked off, go around the top of the inner shell with your pliers and bend down to 90 degree angle. Go by the line marked off. Be sure to bend this "out" from the inside of the circle. Same for the bottom of the inner shell. Bend it "out."

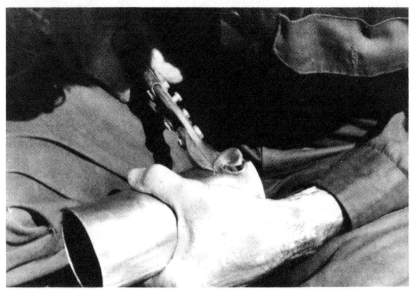

23
King marks outside condenser shell with "condenser stem," then cuts hole for stem.

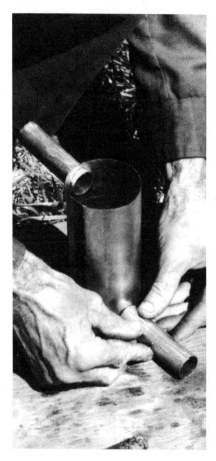

24
Stems are fitted into condenser
outside shell.

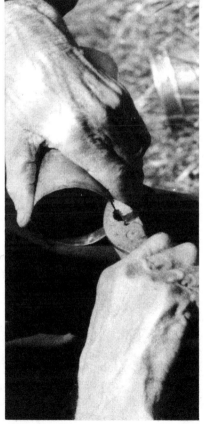

25
Top and bottom of inner shell are bent
"out" from inside.

26
Inner shell is inserted into outer shell of condenser, in preparation for later soldering.

CONNECTIONS

These are vital units that form the vapor line from the still pot to the thump keg to the condenser. They must be cut out and fabricated just as the other pieces of the distillery.

Cap Arm

Thee calls this the cap "stem." It is the connection that runs off of the cap, to carry the vapor over to the thump keg. It is larger on one end than the other. Mark off on your sheet of copper a section seven inches long. On the left end, it is three and one-half inches wide, and on the right end, three inches wide. Mark it off and cut it out. Roll it, in preparation for soldering.

Thump Post

This is called a post, but it is actually a tube. It directs the vapors from the pot down into the thump keg. This section measures 12 inches long and three inches wide. Mark it off and cut it out. Roll it on the large water pipe in preparation for soldering. Set it aside.

Thump Post Top

This provides the right-angle connection between the cap arm and the thump post. It measures 3½ inches long. On the left end, it measures 3½ inches deep, while on the right end, three inches deep. Cut it out and roll it on the water pipe in preparation for soldering. Set it aside.

Headache Piece

This is the connection that comes from the top of the right side of the thump keg. It measures three inches wide and three inches deep. Cut it out, roll it in preparation for soldering.

27
Connection is "rolled" on metal pipe.

Top Slide

This connection links up with the headache piece. It measures four inches long and three inches wide. Cut it out and roll it in preparation for soldering. Set aside.

Bottom Slide

This unit is a wee bit larger than the top slide for a simple reason. It must connect and slide over (for about an inch) the top slide. Measure it out six inches long and 3 and 3/8ths inches wide. This means that when it is rolled and soldered, it will be about one-eighth of an inch bigger in diameter. Roll it in preparation for soldering. Set it aside.

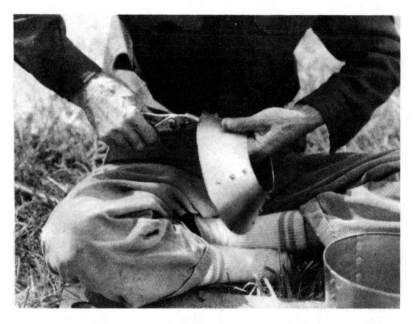

28
Crimp is put around edge of cape to achieve good fit with pot.

29
Cape is placed on pot, with cape seams alternating with pot seams. Next step: spot solder attachment from inside.

Bottom Slide Connector

This connects at a right angle to the bottom slide. It should measure 2½ inches wide. On the left side, it should measure 3 inches top to bottom and on the right side, 2¾ inches. Cut out, roll, and set aside for soldering.

Condenser Stems

One of these connects to the top of the condenser and the other at the bottom. The one at the top is the medium for transporting the vapors into the inner walls of the condenser. The bottom one is the outlet for the condensed liquor. They both measure 3½ inches long and three inches deep. Cut them out, roll them. Set aside in preparation for soldering.

30
Bottom of pot, crimped like a pie crust, is readied for soldering from inside pot.

31
The collar is fitted to cape, then soldered from inside.

SOLDERING

Now you have your entire unit cut out and basically built. The only thing remaining is to get it completely fabricated. You have completed all of the riveting. The only thing that remains is to get the various units soldered and fitted properly.

It is possible that you might want to get the soldering done by a professional. Whether you contract for it to be done by someone else, or whether you do it yourself, here are the steps:

First, you need a roll of acid-core solder. Next, a Coleman gas blow torch soldering unit, fired either with gasoline or LP gas. Get your instructions on soldering from the company that sells the unit to you. The principle of soldering is to heat up the copper at the spot to be soldered, then place the solder on. The solder melts under the intense heat and fuses to the copper at that point.

First when you start to solder, you must have your soldering iron good and hot—the flame having been burning at least 10 minutes.

SOLDERING THE POT TO THE CAPE

You have riveted the copper pot to the cape (top) and to the bottom, but you must solder it, from the inside. You do this by "spot soldering." Place the cape on the pot so that the cape seams alternate with the pot seams. First solder the pot to the cape. Again, make sure you have a snug fit of the cape onto the top of the pot. Then cut one-half inch sections of solder wire. Spot solder the four connections to the cape, inside, where the four lapped and riveted sections of the pot intersect with the cape. Next, make four spot solderings halfway betwen each of the first four solderings. Set aside to cool for a few minutes.

SOLDERING THE BOTTOM OF THE POT

This is going to be a bit ticklish, since you have to push your soldering arm down through the mouth of the cape in order to fuse the round bottom to the pot. First of all, make sure you have an absolute snug fit of the bottom and the pot. Use your hammer and go around the "pie crust" bottom, giving it a few licks all around to make sure the fit is solid. You need to make four spot solderings at the riveted seams. Then you need to solder four additional spots, each of which should be half-way between the original four.

THE COLLAR

Make sure you have a tight, snug fit on this collar. You should solder this all the way around, on the inside. Actually, this collar fits around on the *outside* of the mouth of the cape. Just a bit, perhaps a sixteenth of an inch. But solder the collar on the inside all around its connection to the mouth of the cape.

Now you have your entire pot made, and you can set it aside. On a real working copper pot still—which would be of 30 gallon, 50, 80 or up to 125 gallon capacity—there is another item— a slop arm. This a drain plug to drain the pot after a run. However, on this 2-gallon unit, you can drain the pot by just turning it upside down and pouring out the "pot-tails." So we won't worrry about putting a slop arm on. You might solder one to the bottom as a decoration if you wish. The slop arm in this case would measure one inch in diameter and about four inches long.

THE CAP

This cap has been riveted, so soldering it on the inside is no problem. A little later, we will have another job to do on this cap— cutting in a hole for the cap arm—the one-inch diameter pipe leading to the thump keg. But soldering is the main thing for now. After you have soldered the side of the cap, your big job will be soldering on the top—the big dome that you have beat out. You should have a good fit. Of course, the top edges of the cap wall have been bent inward at a right angle. Check to make sure this has been accomplished. This is important that you get a good fit on this down-bend. Now solder the dome to the cap wall. Solder it carefully all around.

SOLDERING THE CONDENSER

As you have already learned, the two major parts of your condenser are the outer wall and the inner shell. Solder the inner shell first. You should have it rolled and ready for soldering. Lap the left edge over the right edge one-quarter inch and spot solder the seam at the top and bottom. Then solder the entire seam top to bottom. The top and bottom of the shell have been bent out for one-quarter inch. Complete this bending. These bent-out sections will constitute the top and bottom of your condenser when soldered. Put this inside shell aside.

32
Inner and outer shell of condenser are soldered like this.

Now for the outer shell. Solder it the same way as the inner wall. Lap the left edge over the right edge and spot solder at top and bottom. Then solder the entire seam. Now, before you solder the inner shell to the outer shell, you must cut out holes for the condenser connections. Actually, this step comes a bit later, after you have the connections soldered, since you need the connections (pipes) to be used as a pattern for cutting out the holes. But we will go ahead and tell you how at this point, since we are on the subject of the condenser. You need a condenser connection at the top of one side (to bring the vapors into the condenser). You need a similar connection at the bottom to allow the condensed liquid to make its exit.

The bottom pipe is one inch in diameter, and therefore you need to cut out a hole this size for it to fit in. On top, your connection (pipe) is 7/8th of an inch in diameter, so you need to cut out this size for it. First, placing the holes. For the bottom hole, put it about 2½ inches around from the outer shell seam. For the top hole, place it on the exact opposite side. Now each one needs to be about one-fourth of an inch from the top and bottom edges, respectively. To cut these holes, you will need to use your connections for an exact measurement and marking. However, you can use your compass also, by setting it at 7-16ths of an inch for the top and one-half an inch for the bottom. Scribe this circle with your compass and later check it against your connections if you wish to wait until they are fabricated. Use a large nail or chisel to cut enough of a hole to enable you to "hook" it with your shears. Then use the shears to cut out the hole. Both top and bottom.

Your next job on the condenser is fitting the inner shell into the outer shell. The inner shell, of course, has a quarter inch bend-out, top and bottom, so it may take a bit of doing to get it fitted inside the outer shell. But when you get it in, be sure to set the inner shell seam on the opposite side of the outer shell. When you have satisfied yourself that you have a good fit, solder the inner shell to the outer shell, top and bottom. This requires soldering all around to achieve a tight closure.

Put aside your condenser for the moment. You can fabricate the connections later.

33

The double-wall condenser walls are soldered, top and bottom. Vapors go through the inside of the two walls in condensation.

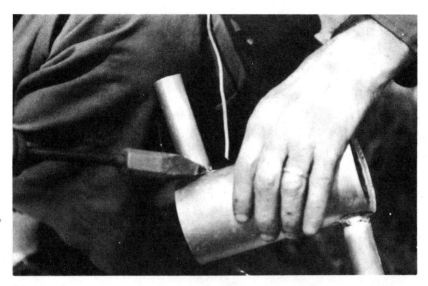

34
Stems are soldered onto condenser.

FABRICATING THE CONNECTIONS

There are eight connections that must be fabricated with solder.

First of all, there is the cap arm. You already have it rolled and ready. So solder it from one end to the other. Now before you solder this cap arm to the cap, you must cut out the hole for the connection. Locate this hole on the side of the cap, right at the top of the seam. This means when you cut out this hole, you will cut out one of the rivets. Don't worry. That's the way it's done. First of all, measure the diameter of your cap arm. It should measure about an inch and a quarter at the big end . . . the end that must connect with the cap. Using your compass, scribe this circle. Now take your cap arm and place it at the spot to double check the cut needed. Now use your shears and cut out the hole. Place the end of the cap arm onto the hole in the cap. Solder all around the outside so that you get a solid fabrication.

Now comes time to solder the remaining connections. Roll and solder,

—The thump post top.

—The thump post.

—The headache piece.

—The top slide.
—The bottom slide.
—The bottom slide connector, and
—Condenser stems.

When you have completed these jobs, you are now getting close to completion. But not yet. First of all, on your Thump Post, you need to cut the bottom at a 90-degree angle. You can do this with your shears. This enables the vapors to make a speedy exit in the bottom of the thump. Now cut the Thump Post top at a 90-degree angle. You do the same thing for the small end of the Thump Post top. This is so that these two pieces can be soldered at a right angle. Solder these two pieces all around the connection.

35
Thee King is not playing a tune. He's checking the air-tightness of his new double wall condenser.

36
Thump post is cut by tin snips for 90-degree angle connection.

Now cut the right end of your headache piece at about a 100-degree angle. The same for the top slide. Solder these two pieces together. Make sure it is a good, solid solder.

Now cut the bottom of the bottom slide at a 30-degree angle. Do the same thing with the large end of the bottom slide connector. Now solder these two pieces.

Condenser arms (or connections). There are two of these, one for the top and one for the bottom. Place them onto the outer shell of the condenser and solder them around the outside, leaving a good solid solder seam.

To make sure your condenser is good and tight, put your hand tightly over the bottom connection and blow into the top. Or you can pour water into it. You can tell if you have a leak. If so, put some additional solder on.

For all essential purposes, your still has been completed. Check to make sure your thump post fits down into the thump keg okay. The bottom of the thump post—cut off at the 90-degree angle—should come almost to the bottom of the keg.

Also, you'll want to check your flake stand, the wooden box, to find the proper place to bore holes for the condenser arms.

37
Thump post is connected and soldered.

THE OPERATION OF YOUR STILL

The principle of a distillery of whiskey is this: Alcohol vaporizes at 173 degrees. So you want to heat it not much over this amount. So you need to figure a way to heat your pot so that it goes not much over 180 degrees.

This will enable the still to extract the alcoholic essence from the liquid mash. The next step is for your condenser to condense the hot vapors back into liquid—distilled liquor.

And, of course, the principle here is to cool the vapors as efficiently as possible. Old timers always piped cool water into the flake stand to cool the vapors. You could do this, or you could fill your flake stand with ice. Pack it all around the condenser.

As to heating for the pot, you could use a hot plate, or you could set it up in some sort of a rock furnace like the old timers did.

In any event, you fill your pot with the mash—or distiller's beer. To obtain the *second* distillation on the one run, you should fill up your thump keg about one-third full of distiller's beer. The hot vapors coming from the pot will achieve this.

If you do not wish to use the thumper keg, you can run the hot vapors from the pot directly into the condenser. Of course, what you have is "low wines"—or singlings. And you will have to take what you get from six or eight "runs" of singlings and put it into the pot for a "doubling run." You avoid all this when you use a thump keg, which is called by many people a "doubler."

So there you have it. This is the way Thee King builds a small distillery unit. But remember, if you actually distill mash into whiskey, you are breaking the federal law.

So, after you have built your still, think long and hard before you fire it up.

38

Theodore King holds still he has just completed. The pot and connections are in his right hand, and the condenser is in the left.

Chapter
7

A B C's of Stilling

A young East Tennessean enrolled as a student in
metal-working with the International Correspondence
School, but after sending in several assignments
promptly, his reports aburuptly stopped. A few weeks
later, ICS received a letter from him—postmarked the
state prison. He asked they not judge him too harshly.
He reported that in his trial, the DA brought his whiskey
still in the courtroom as evidence. The judge and jury
"all thought it was the finest copperwelding job they
had ever seen and I owe it all to the ICS."

A B C's of Stilling

Forty-five crooked miles from Atlanta's Perimeter Highway in the rolling Appalachian foothills of North Georgia, the bulldozers of progress may one day smash through what was at one time Georgia's finest moonshine reservoir. Thousand of acres of hardwood forests and bold streams, once honeycombed with illicit copper pot stills and larger "stack steamers" and commercial boiler distilleries, lie directly in the growth pattern of Atlanta. The city possesses ten thousand Dawson County acres and also has under option several thousand acres of land in Paulding County, another one of the old-time moonshine producing areas.

Once Georgia's moonshiningest region, these counties are wild, woodsy and sparsely settled, and were an ideal haunt for illicit whiskey making from the 1800's to a few years ago. The encroachment of the big city is spelling the final doom to its skilled illicit whiskey artisans who are already on their last legs. Hundreds of North Georgia moonshiners either are "building time" in United States penitentiaries or have already served time. Many others have had generous educational experiences with the ever present and efficient "Big Law"—Treasury Department's Bureau of Alcohol, Tobacco and Firearms people, known respectfully among illicit whiskey makers everywhere as "the revenue," and among some as "the federal law."

Dawson County's old moonshiners, who remember the glorious freedom they had of roaming its hills and fording its streams without being "crowded," are not happy. Among them is an 84-year-old ex-moonshiner.

"I'd hate to see that airport in Dawson County," he told me. "You couldn't hear yourself fart."

To Sam Jones, we'll call him, now living out his days in a rest home in a neighboring county, moonshining was a way of life which is now fading off of the American screen. "Everybody nearly made liquor back then. That's the only way you could make anything. Didn't have no way of gettin' hold of a dime unless you made liquor."

As a teen-ager, Sam cooked up his first batch of booze on a branch back out behind his daddy's corn field. "Me and another boy decided we'd try to make a run on a coffee pot. I had watched my pap make it. We rigged that coffee pot up with pipes and spouts. We made a mash out of cornbread. Crumbled it up and mashed it in. We made a pint in all day a Sunday, besides what we drunk."

Sam's use of the coffee pot illustrates how very simple distilling can be (yet still very much unlawful). But the spread between the coffee pot still and today's modern legal distilleries represents a wide range in distilling technology.

In this chapter, we want to take up types of stills and appurtenances.

TYPES OF STILLS

A complete breakdown of the illegal stills operated by American moonshiners over the years would fill a catalogue. But for openers, consider . . . submarine, ground hog (or hog), jimbuck, silver cloud, old yellow, black pot, blue kettle, coffin (or dead man), grey ghost, pan, stack steamer, blockade, column, buccaneer, and, of course, the copper pot. To extend our inquiry a bit, consider such still appurtenances as thump rod, headache piece, flake stand, dry relay, worm, slop arm, money piece, thumper keg (or doubler), puke barrel, shotgun condenser and bird cage condenser.

These are all part of moonshining lore and most of the pieces of equipment they represent are still in use today across the South wherever the production of white whiskey is pursued with vigor and determination. The style and variation of an illicit distillery setup varies considerably from area to area and from moonshiner to moonshiner. The basic components of a distillery are, (1), the fermenting equipment; (2), the distilling equipment, and (3), the condensing equipment. But many stills have a lot of extras, more or less according to the taste of the maker. Where moonshiners ply their trade, their improvisations are a sight to behold. "Every moonshiner has his own style," is a valid statement heard across the South.

Virtually all of the illicit stills operating in recent years in the South are classified by the ATF as pot-type distilleries.

Thee King (R) and friend put together galvanized upright pot still at First Annual Appalachian Ex-Moonshiners & Revenuers Convention.

The pot type distillery consists of a metal and/or wood still "in the form of a pot, kettle, box, drum or barrel." These pot stills produce whiskey when fire is applied directly to a surface of the still, with the exception of the steamer type where the mash is vaporized by steam fed into the pot by pipes.

Some pot stills are used only for distillation of mash that is femented in separate mash containers. These are primarily the copper and metal pots. In another type—primarily the Alabama Pot Type (sometimes known as Black Pots), and Groundhog— the mash is fermented and distilled in the same container. This is also true of the Silver Cloud stills of East Tennessee, as well as the Submarine style of North Carolina.

We might point out that "stills" refers to the pot, or kettle, only, while "distillery" refers to an entire whiskey-making outfit. Here is a breakdown of basic still types:

Copper Pot

This most ancient of stills—with its roots going back to Scotland and Ireland—was the overwhelming favorite of the Appalachian frontiersman from Pennsylvania to Arkansas, and can still be found in some small, isolated operations through the mountains of the Southeast.

The copper pot "mother still" is found in three configurations —the "turnip," round and fat; the "half turnip," and the upright copper pot, shaped like a metal drum and placed vertically in the furnace. It is also called the Buccaneer, the Blockade Still and the "mountain teapot." The American copper pot is very similar to the "poit du" (black pot) stills on display in the Highland Folk Museum in Scotland and the Poteen stills in Ireland. This still, made of copper throughout, is heated from the bottom by a firebox with the flames and smoke exiting the rear. It has a single chamber, a still-head (or cap), and an arm leading to a worm condenser, set in a water-filled flake stand (known in Scotland as a "worm tub").

The American version is very similar, but ingenious distillers of the Appalachians years ago came up with a method to cook the mash without burning or scorching the meal that settles to the bottom. They accomplished this by building a double walled bottom surface. Later, they came up with an even better method, which also "burned up the smoke" by circulating it completely around, over and back up to and out the front of the still. They

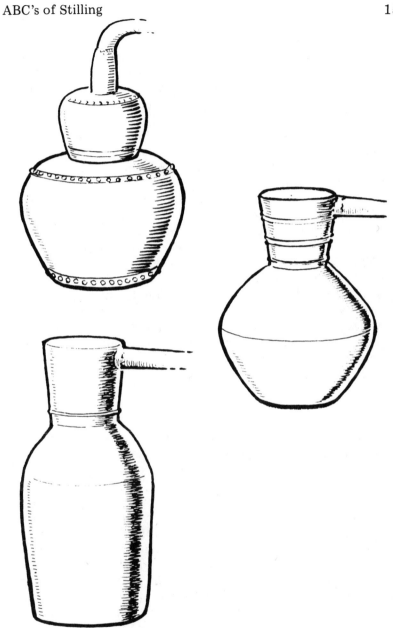

The Mother Still of the Appalachians, the copper pot. It comes in three basic types, the round "turnip" type, the "half turnip," and the upright copper pot. (Sketches by Tom Hill)

achieved this by placing over the front of the furnace a thick bed rock (and in later years sections of railroad tracks). But they left an opening at the back so that the flames could lap back up and over the bed rock, around both sides of the pot, or kettle, and out through an opening in the front. Such stills draw flames "like a blow torch." To prevent heat loss, the distillers built up a firebox of fieldstone chinked with mud around the sides, back and front, closing over the still at the cape. This is called a "stump furnace," a "duck nest," a "bedrock furnace," and sometimes an "eyebrow singer." "Any good 'shiner could put his overall jumper under a pot (over the bedrock), and it would never scorch," a state revenuer recalled. Through this method, distillers avoided scorching the beer. The copper pot still, also known as the "blockade," "buccaneer," or "turnip type" variety, ranged in capacity from 10 gallons to 100 gallons. Many of the "copper pot craftsmen" soldered connections with silver solder, although most stills were so tight-fitting, they did not require soldering, being put together with rivets and brads on crimped edges.

On top of the still pot proper is a copper "cap," in which the alcohol vapors collect before moving on toward the condenser. Moonshiners traditionally have sealed up the cap-pot connection with rye or wheat paste, giving it a cement-like sealant.

Metal Pot

The ATF defines the metal pot still as being one constructed of any metal other than copper—no matter what shape or size—which is heated by direct application of fire. Many moonshiners in recent years have resorted to metals other than copper in building their stills—primarily tin, galvanized iron and, in some cases aluminum. But aluminum stills are relatively scarce. Copper carries with it the image among distillers (rightfully so) of being the perfect metal, both for conducting heat and for resisting corrosion. Unlike some other metals or alloys, copper withstands the effects of the alcohol and does not corrode. In addition, it is light and tough. One ex-moonshiner in Rabun County, Georgia, declared that he unfortunately did not get to make all his stills out of copper. "A few times I used sheet iron, for the simple reason that I was too durned poor to buy copper. But I always used copper connections, and I always made sure to leave the pot filled with something, if nothing but water, to keep it from rusting between runs. If you emptied it out, it would rust like nobody's business.

The late Peg Fields.

Lot of people run 'em with rust in it. But when my still would rust when we moved it from one place to another, we would take sand and ashes and scour that thing out just as clean . . . ."

Silver Clouds

This is one of the unique, localized versions of the metal pot still. It is common in east Tennessee, centered in the area around Cosby in the shadow of the Great Smoky Mountain National Park. From a valley below, the "Cosby Silver Cloud" is said to resemble a cloud. They are cylindrical pots made of galvanized steel, with heat being applied by burners through single or twin flues through the lower third of the pot. Up to the 1950's, the Cosby moonshiners utilized copper for these stills, but this proved too expensive since they were losing so many to dynamiting by ATF agents. They resorted to the galvanized metal units, which they could buy, pre-cut, for around $40. These stills—which are used for fermenting mash as well as distilling it—are enormous in size—up to 1,000 gallons in capacity.

Another type of metal pot—popular along "Tobacco Road" near Augusta, Ga., was a "steel drum still." 'Stillers welded drums together, end to end. Usually two or three were put together, but sometimes as many as four. They laid these down horizontally over the furnace, and cut a hole in the top for the cap, and usually ran a galvanized pipe directly to a condenser.

Groundhog

This still—sometimes called a "hog"—is usually found dug into the side of a hill or bank (usually next to a stream). It is usually a huge metal cylinder with a wooden top and bottom. It is set up vertically in a bank with about two feet of space between its walls and the surrounding bank. Its wooden bottom is placed about a foot or two underneath the ground, to prevent it from being burned. The furnace for the groundhog is the air space around and outside the cylinder. The fire is placed next to the pot on the front. The flames wrap around it on either side, and exit at the top on the backside. This is sometimes called a "tail furnace." The heat chamber is covered all around on top with sheet metal, weighted with soil, almost level with the surrounding ground surface. A hole is cut right in the center of the wooden top, and onto this is placed the cap—sometimes a 50-gallon wooden keg, sometimes a metal drum and, on rare occasions, a hand-crafted copper cap. Developed in the 1930's, the groundhog still has a lot more capacity than most copper or metal pots, but its key difference is that, in addition to its greater capacity, it serves as both the fermenting pot as well as the distilling pot. Moreover, there is greater heat efficiency since more of the still's surface is in contact with the fire. A groundhog can be square, round, tall or long.

In recent years, some moonshiners, particularly in South Georgia and Florida, have described hugh metal tank type stills as "hogs,"—some of which are heated from the metal underside and some from a flue or pipe which extends through the tank. But this is an inaccurate description. However, for those tanks with wooden bottoms, which are heated from the side, the "hog" description would be valid.

Alabama Pot Type

This is a cylindrical still very similar in size and shape to the groundhog. It has a wooden top and bottom, and metal sides. But

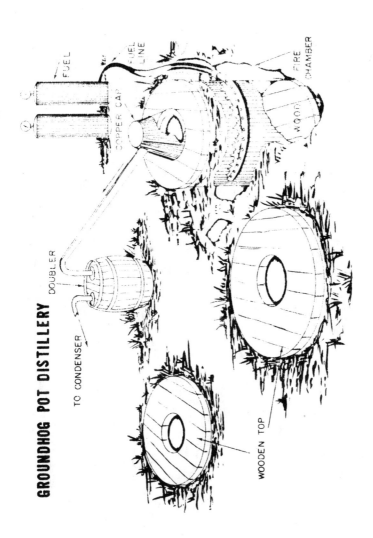

GROUNDHOG POT DISTILLERY

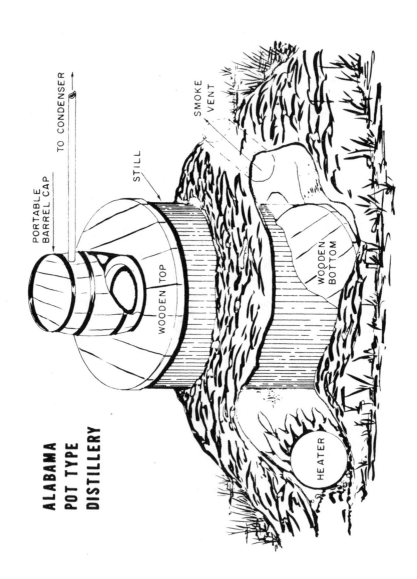

ALABAMA
POT TYPE
DISTILLERY

PORTABLE BARREL CAP

TO CONDENSER

STILL

SMOKE VENT

WOODEN TOP

WOODEN BOTTOM

HEATER

it is placed on the ground surface, with its wooden bottom buried only enough to prevent burning. A furnace is built above ground, with the fire chamber surrounding the midsection of the still. Across northern Alabama, in the Cumberland Plateau area of Tennessee and in the Tennessee River Valley area north of Chattanooga, this type still is called the "Black Pot." Moonshiner Hamper McBee described it this way: "You put an old pot in the ground and you put your mash and everything right in the pot and build your fire around it and that's what they call a duck nest. You just build your furnace around your pot." He declares, "You can make more money with a black pot outfit (than a steamer) 'cause sometimes you can get fourteen, fifteen gallons out of a 100-gallon batch on a pot when you might get ten gallons out of an average run on a steam outfit, unless they add in the backins."

Some of the black pots have tremendous capacities, up to and in some cases more than a thousand gallons. Old time copper pot craftsmen looked with scorn at the introduction of the black pots and would declare in contempt, "He makes *black pot likker*."

Submarine

This is a rectangular still which is usually built on a wooden frame, with the metal wrapped around the frame on the bottom, and in some cases on the ends and top. Its sides are built of wood. Found primarily in the eastern Carolinas, Virginia and south Georgia, they are heated either by a coke-fed fire or by fuel oil or butane gas. The name submarine was attached to the still long ago when moonshiners dug them deep into hillsides. However, most are now found erected on level ground without too much digging.

Pan

Similar in appearance to the submarine, most pan stills are solid metal, usually welded steel or iron. Most are huge rectangular, box-like containers, made of quarter-inch sheet iron which is completely sealed up except for a two-foot diameter hole in the top for the cap. The mash is fermented and cooked right in the same container. However, in some push-button operations, the sugar and water are mixed at nearby buildings and pumped into the box where the other ingredients, such as grain meal, malt and yeast, are then added. The caps are usually half of a 55-gallon metal drum.

Although most are solid metal boxes, some have plywood sides and tops. Most of the pan-type stills in North Georgia measure four or six feet wide, eight or ten feet long and four to six feet tall, with a capacity of from 800 to 2,250 gallons. In south Georgia, the sizes are somewhat larger, up to 3,000 gallons capacity. Most big pan-type distilleries will have a number of pans, so the pans can be distilled in sequence. An outfit with three 1800-gallon pans would rotate every three days, since it requires three days for the fermentation. A huge pan-type distillery complex destroyed by the ATF in south Georgia had five pans which were distilled simultaneously. Each tank had two bottles of butane gas supplying its heat. The pans, measuring four feet deep, four feet wide and eight feet long, held 960 gallons of mash. When seized, all five tanks were distilling whiskey at the same time, utilizing "rat tail" jet type burner. "With those five rat-tails going plus the pumps, it sounded like the flight line at the Atlanta airport," an agent recalled. Each tank had as a cap a 55-gallon metal drum. Galvanized stove pipes led from the five caps into a giant "shotgun" condenser, containing 50 copper tubes, to carry the vapor through the water-filled jacket. This operation, typical of the modern-day stills, required eight to ten "still hands" to keep it running. In some moonshine distilling complexes, there will be a series of such tanks, with one condenser, and each of the tanks is distilled in succession, by hooking on to the condenser, usually a shotgun type. A variation of the pan still is the "Coffin Still," which is sealed in with a domed top like a coffin.

Steamer

The steamer is a pot still utilizing steam to cook the mash. The steam producing unit may consist of a home-made steel drum boiler—sometimes known as a "stack steamer" or a "double drum steamer"—or a commercially produced high pressure or low pressure boiler. Some home-made steamers have utilized metal drums laid over a furnace horizontally. The still pot itself may be built of wood, and many of them are built this way, particularly the "Wilkesboro type" in the North Carolina Piedmont. The Wilkesboro steamer distilling pot consists of a stave-type barrel, into which the steam from the boiler is piped, to vaporize the alcohol. The distilling pot can be a wooden barrel, box or drum. The steamer type still creates a tremendous rhythmic pounding in its "thump keg" when it begins distilling. A north Georgia moon-

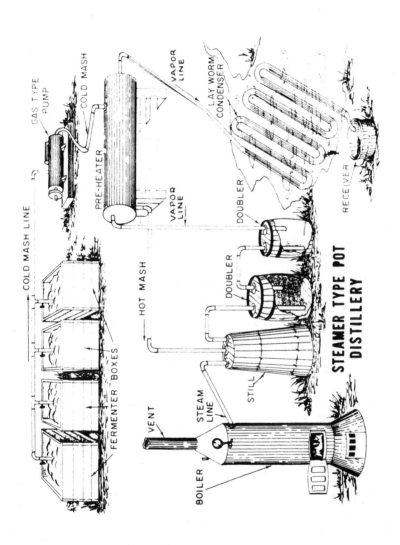

STEAMER TYPE POT DISTILLERY

shiner declares that "When that hot steam comes out and hits that cold beer, it just rumbles back through there. Sounds like somebody beating on a 55-gallon barrel with a hammer. You can hear it a mile away . . . boom . . . boom . . . boom. One time my still made such an awful racket, I ran out and kicked all the dogs and started up my old cars. I had three or four cars. You could still hear it. I laid a big old rock on top of that thump keg. After it got to thumpin' good, it simmered down and just sat there and quivered. You couldn't hear it then."

Snuffy Smith's neighbor: "Can I have
some of your squeezins?"
Snuffy: "What's wrong with your own?"
Neighbor: "Oh, nothing, I just get
tired of my own cookin!"

Some of the home-made steamers have been quite dangerous, particularly those built without pop-off valves, or water pressure gauges. Many such boilers have exploded, causing injury to still hands. One such still, located on an island in the Potomac River near the nation's capital, blew up during Prohibition days, maiming several workers. A steamer explosion on Tennessee's Cumberland plateau burned a worker. He grabbed a foot tub full of high-proof whiskey and poured it over his body. It left him with a solid blister over his back but he refused to see a doctor and eventually recuperated. The home-made steamers consist of two or three 55-gallon drums welded together, with reinforcement added to the bottom drum. They can be set into the furnace either vertically or horizontally. The early stack steamers were fired with coke and had grates in the bottom. A brick furnace was built up around the stack. In some operations, two 220-gallon olive barrels were placed together to form the distilling pot. In other cases, moonshiners would put a 100-gallon wooden barrel on the bottom and "cap" it with a 60-gallon keg, which gave a capacity of one hundred and forty gallons of beer.

Before we leave still types. something should be said about the still cap, an important part of each distillery setup. The alcohol vapors collect in this cap before moving on toward the condensers. Always detachable from the pot and usually fabricated to a "cap arm," caps range from the copper domes that fit down into a copper pot to a half or a full 55-gallon drum, or, in some cases, a wooden keg. A craftsman still maker on Signal Mountain, Tennessee, said, "the bigger the cap, the better the still. With a little cap, a lot of impurities can get through." Old time distillers in Scotland felt the same way, crediting fine quality whiskey to the shape of the "head," which affected the proportion of fusel oils reaching the condenser.

CONDENSERS

The next basic area where there is considerable variety is in the condensing equipment. At small distilleries, the condenser is usually the most expensive piece of equipment. 'Stillers quickly whisk their "worm" to safekeeping on word of an imminent raid. Condensers usually are set in a box or barrel, called a "flake stand," into which cool water is constantly pumped. Sometimes they are laid down flat in streams. The principle is to apply as much cool temperature to the condensing surface as possible and to insure that the whiskey pouring out of the end is "real cool." If it is hot it will evaporate, and also will have a bad taste.

Here is a breakdown of basic condenser types:

Copper Coil

Known usually as the "worm," this is the old stand-by condenser, which was used in Scotland and Ireland in the 1500's and is still considered quite efficient. Copper tubing, usually an inch or an inch and a half in diameter, is shaped like a coil, usually being bent around a tree stump, while filled with sand or pine rosin. The bottom end of the coil protrudes from the flake stand and from this, the liquor pours into a receiving container.

Lay-Worm, or Branch Type

A number of equal lengths of copper tubing are joined by copper angle pipes and laid horizontally in a rectangular cooler box or in a stream of water which is built up with a dam so that the receiving tank can be placed at the open end of the worm to collect the distilled liquor. Some of these condensers would measure eight to twelve feet across, from one side to the other.

Earl Palmer

Get you a copper kettle
Get you a copper coil
Get you some new-made
    corn mash
and never more will you toil . . . .
        Old Mountain verse.

Automobile or Truck Radiator

An increasingly popular condenser innovation in recent years, the radiator is used singly or a number in tandem, joined by connecting pipes. This type condenser can be submerged vertically or horizontally in a flake stand or in a stream. The first radiators used in the early 1900's performed very well. They were made out of brass and copper, were free of rust, and did not have antifreeze in them. In recent years, however, ATF investigators have found that solder used in repairing damaged radiators has been the largest single contributor of poisonous lead salts in moonshine whiskey.

Shotgun Type

Being found more and more at the huge, pushbutton type illicit distilleries, the shotgun condenser, sometimes called the gatling gun type, is a cylindrical copper water jacket which looks a lot like an Army bazooka gun and measures from six feet to 20 feet long. It contains many small copper tubes—sometimes as many as 50—through which the vapors travel. The jacket is sealed and has a water intake area usually at the back end of the unit. The water circulates through the jacket and exits at the front.

Sleeve-Type

This condenser has a copper tube running lengthwise through a cylindrical tank, which has a continuous flow of cold water through it. A variation of this is what is known as a "double wall" condenser in which the vapors are condensed within the double-walled unit, with cold water flowing on both sides of the vapors, which travel within these double wall.

There are many variations in the condensers, based on improvisations by the 'shiners. There is a "bird cage," in which copper tubes shaped in the form of a bird cage, with all the tubes coming together at the bottom where the whisky comes out into the container. The bird cage is merely kept submerged in a container of cold water. There is a "star" condenser, shaped like an elongated star. The point of the condenser is to obtain as much cool temperature to the surface of the fixture. There is a "muffler" condenser which shaped like an automobile muffler.

The condenser is set in a water circulating box or a barrel, known as a "flake stand," or sometimes laid out in a flowing stream. The idea is to apply as much cool temperature as possible to the condensing surface.

FERMENTERS AND APPURTENANCES

Fermenting containers represent the third basic piece of distillery equipment, and are called "fermenters," "mash pots," "mash barrels," "mash boxes," or "mash vats."

In the early days of grain whiskey making in the Appalachians—up to and through Prohibition days—the common mash container was the wooden barrel of from 50 to 150 gallons capacity. These were usually hand made on the farm of white oak, with hickory strip hoops holding them tight, with notched "latches." In case the moonshiner could not afford the barrels, he would fashion mash containers out of hollow gum logs, by attaching a head on one end. It was called a "gum" and was the same type used to hive bees. A moonshiner recalled that "back then, we just didn't have the durn money to buy barrels with. You could buy a second hand barrel for seventy-five cents to a dollar. But you couldn't get the 75 cents to git it with. So we'd just cut good well-seasoned poplar or chestnut lumber. Most all the chestnut trees were dead but a lot of the logs were still sound as a dollar. We made three by three by three foot boxes." Some moonshiners in the 1930's used 220-gallon used olive and pickle barrels, which were common also in North Carolina in the 1950's. Many distillers, particularly in the mountains, buried their mash barrels, leaving the top flush with the ground. This was especially helpful in the winter, when insulation was needed to maintain an adequate temperature. "We had a still one time on the quarry hill," a Rabun County, Georgia, man told me, "and we buried twenty barrels. We got rye straw and hay and packed it around them. It was a pretty severe winter, but the mash 'kicked over' in five or six days." The same moonshiner found buried mash barrels were a good insurance against excessive heat in the summer time. Too much heat will cause wild yeast "vinegar mother" to form on top. "If that forms, you might as well throw away your mash. It's vinegar by then."

In recent years, ATF raiders have found huge fermenting vats at still sites—usually big metal or wooden boxes, with huge capacities to accommodate big production distilling rigs. Some of the modern day illicit stills have 600-gallon "wrap around" fermenters.

These are very similar to ground hog stills in that they have wooden heads and wooden bottoms, with galvanized steel wrap-around sides. The mash is pumped from these containers into the still pot.

There are many "add-ons" that moonshiners place on their distilling rigs besides the basic fermenter, still pot and condenser.

The Thump Keg

Just about the most common addition is the "thump keg," or thumper, (sometimes called the "thump chest" or doubler), usually a 55-gallon barrel or steel drum, which is placed between the distilling kettle and the condenser. It thumps like crazy at the beginning of a run. By filling this keg part way up with distiller's beer, or low-proof whiskey called "backins" from a previous run, the thumper serves as a "doubler," giving the whiskey a second distillation, making it "doubled" whiskey without a second run.

Hamper McBee at cave still site in Tennessee.

Copper pot still set up at the First Annual Appalachian Ex-Moonshiners and Revenuers Convention is put into operation by ex-moonshiner Thee King of Blairsville, Georgia. Here he simulates stirring in a batch of distillers beer (fermented mash) in the pot itself, prior to "capping down" with the cap on the ground at left. In center is the "thump keg"—which is a doubler. From there, the vapor line runs into the pre-heater box (top left) and down to the "flake stand" at lower left in which a copper coil condenser is located.

King remembers making corn whiskey in the mountains of Towns County in the 1930's. "In 1932, in Hoover Days, we were selling likker for

90 cents a gallon. We'd take wagon loads to Murphy, North Carolina. Sell it in sixty-gallon barrels, and bring back hundred-pound sacks of sugar for $3.98 a sack. We had Model A Fords and wagons. But getting whiskey out of the hills, we used mostly sleds. And we rawhided it out of the mountains on our backs. I've carried many a kag of liquor six and eight miles on my back.

"In the pure corn days, we'd make twelve and a half gallons of likker to the acre. Course, we also had our bread corn out of that and we'd feed our mules out of it."

The alcoholic vapors from the still are piped to the bottom of the thumper keg. The heat from this causes a distillation from the surface of the mash, out a second pipe at the top of the keg. The vapors then travel to the condenser. Some stills have a series of these kegs—some of them dry—to serve as "cleaning barrels," or "filter kegs," or "slobber kegs," to pick up excess water or meal. "There's where you make your clear likker," a moonshiner told me. "If it pukes, it comes out milky as the devil." Another purpose of the thumper keg is to help cool down the vapors before they reach the condenser. A North Georgia operator told me, "To make good licker, on the first run, you use beer to charge that thumper. On the second run, when your licker gets to running about 70 proof, you turn your fire off, because you've got about all you're going to get out of that run. The last five gallons will be about 50 proof—'backins' they call it. Use that in your thumper keg on the second run, instead of beer, and you'll get better licker."

Some operators place a "dry relay"—an empty barrel—horizontally next to the still pot, to catch mash that belches into the line with the vapors before being distilled. This barrel is set up to be lower on the end toward the still, with a pipe leading from the bottom of the barrel back into the still pot. This enables the operator to let the mash back into the pot for the next run.

The Preheater

Just about the most efficient add-on to a still—a development since the turn of the century—is the preheater. A wooden box with a capacity about the size of the still pot, it usually is placed relatively close to the still pot, and at a higher elevation. The alcoholic vapors on the way to the condenser are piped through a double-walled tube through this pre-heater, heating up the mash for the next run. This also serves to help cool down the vapors. A trough is attached to the box, to enable the operator to gravity feed the pre-heated mash into the still for the next run.

Recitifier

As the clear, white whiskey comes out of the condenser, moonshiners usually strain the product to clean it of impurities. Just to what extent the operator goes to do this depends on the type moonshiner you have. A cornlicker craftsman usually would get some hickory charcoals, wash them, and put them in the straining funnel, along with cloth at the top and the bottom. The typical straining device for many years was and still is the old felt "moonshiner hat." Some operators—particularly in the Cumberland Plateau of Tennessee—build elaborate rectifiers. Here's how one ex-moonshiner described his. He took a 10-gallon keg. On the bottom, he placed a layer of white woolen cloth. On top of that, he poured in two inches of white sand. On top of that was placed another layer of white woolen cloth. From there to the top of the keg, he placed sugar maple charcoal. "It takes five gallons to prime it, and your wiskey comes out clear as hell," he declared. Another operator said some people buy whiskey raw, rectify it and are able to get a $2 per gallon premium.

Tempering Barrel

This is sometimes called a "blending tub." Usually it is a container large enough for the operator to mix up his entire run. The high proof "high shots" from the early part of the run must be blended with the lower proof liquor that comes out later to give a uniform proof. "When it first starts runnin' (on a steam rig)," an operator declared, "it's about a hundred and eighty proof. About pure alcohol. As Uncle Rufe says, when you taste that you got ahold of sumpin' you can't drink. Can't get your breath. That's a hundred and eighty proof. When you get it all run off you'll have about a hundred and twenty proof liquor and when you put in in the keg you'll still have a hundred and at least fourteen or fifteen." Another operator declared that a groundhog still turns out a lower proof whiskey. "You want to leave it about a hundred and five proof. If you want to cut it, you can, with water. If it's running close, it don't take much water. You can take a handful of water and kill 20 gallons of licker. Just knock it out. If you cut it too low, you have to go back and use beading oil in it. That's a highly-refined cooking oil. Sells for $20 a gallon. Just takes a drop or two per gallon. It's powerful."

FUEL FOR THE DISTILLERY

The prime fuel for stills for many years—particularly during the copper pot era—was wood. During the era of lax law enforcement, pioneers would establish a still and would clean off the hardwood from the hillsides around it. Revenooers could tell how

This groundhog still has a 50-gallon keg on top as the cap. An ex-moonshiner in Cherokee County, Georgia, described how he made a "five sacker hog" (a groundhog still with a capacity of five 100-pound sacks of sugar— 500 gallons of mash). He called this size still "just big enough to get you in trouble. I wouldn't mess with one myself; it's not big enough. If you're going to make liquor, make liquor— build one that will run a stream of whiskey as big as a broom handle." Despite his distaste for the inadequate size of the 500-gallon ground-hog, he described the construction steps this way: "You buy a 4 x 8 or a 4 x 10 foot piece of aluminum, tin, or galvanized iron and roll it up. Then you get tongue and groove 2 x 6's and nail them together for the bottom and the top. These must be cut in the form of a circle, four feet in diameter. Lay these sections in the water for several days and they'll swell and won't leak a drop. When you start to nail your metal sheet onto the side of the top and bottom pieces, tear off strips of a bed sheet and place it between the wooden top and the metal. Nail it down with roofing nails." Several 2 x 4's are used as bracers around the inside of the still wall. A hole is then cut into the top for the placement of the cap, usually a 50-gallon barrel. "Your burner goes in front and it's a wraparound burner," my informant declared. "The best thing is to use fuel oil and gas, mixed half and half . . . makes the hottest far (fire) a-tall." (Also, with this mixture, there is less danger of an explosion than with 100 per cent gas).

Old time copper pot distillery set up deep in the laurels in Lumpkin County, Georgia, in the early 1900's. The copper cooker is situated on top of the furnace to the right of the man with the axe. The mash barrels situated about are hand made, with notched hickory bands. Man at right holds a hand-made "mash stick," sometimes called a "stir stick." It is a hardwood pole about six feet long, with pegs inserted in the end to enable the distiller to stir and comb the lumps out of the mash. Man squatting in center holds a tiny proof vial in which samples of freshly-run whiskey would be taken periodically to test the proof. Whiskey proofing out at 100 proof would contain 50 per cent alcohol. The 50-gallon keg laying in front with the bung tapped in probably was full of fresh whiskey ready to be hauled off to a nearby thirsty market. (Photo courtesy Mrs. Madeleine Anthony).

This is a "submarine" type distillery, found mostly in North Carolina and Southwest Virginia. This unit holds about 290 gallons of mash and—with a slow fire underneath—will spout about a pint of likker per minute through the copper worm in the box-like "flake stand" at left. The first shots of this "doubled" whiskey (note the "thump keg" doubler in middle) will be about 160 proof alcohol, very "beady," or "frog-eyed." Last whiskey out is low in alcohol and is called "backins" and sometimes "drapping the bead." When the bead drops, the distiller prepares to "set-back" the spent mash, with the addition of sugar and malt, for another run. Many connoisseurs of corn whiskey consider this "slopping back"—particularly the first sour-mash run—to yield the best drinking likker. Even the photographer of this picture admits he likes this stage of whiskey. "The first sugar," as Earl Palmer describes it.

long a still had been operating by the amount of trees logged off a mountain. Later, when efforts were made to keep stills hidden from the eyes of the law, wood was sought which would give off the least amount of smoke. Many felt green ash was the best, although others chose locust. Green ash, declared an old timer, "just lays there and fries and don't make no racket or no smoke." Locust was known for its limited amount of smoke but hickory was popular because it was said to provide the hottest fire, and its ashes produced the best lye, which some 'shiners used to hurry along fermentation, or to clean out the inside of the still after a

After a "run" is completed, the expensive copper "worm" and "cap" are toted away along with the fresh likker, which is hidden in a secret stash, sometimes buried in the ground, sometimes placed in hollow stumps. Man in right foreground carries a five-gallon can of "single-foot" (single distilled moonshine) which he'll hide in nearby laurel thickets awaiting sale. Man in center carries the worm and cap.

Earl Palmer

run. In most cases, long logs of hardwood were fed into a furnace steadily during a run.

With the advent of the steamer, coke was used. A former moonshiner along the Etowah River north of Cartersville, Georgia, remembered going to Atlanta to pick up coke. "They knowed what you were going to do with it. They used to be a little old place down on Decatur Street there, just off a little side street about a half block off Decatur, that we bought our coke and our sugar, brown sugar, from a Jew. Just a little hole in the wall. This little bitty place. We'd haul it in cars. We'uza loading it up there and a police was there and he says, 'It goes out dry and comes back shakin'.' And the Jew says, 'No, no, no. This man runs a big bakery.'"

Since World War II, fuel oil and lp gas have been the favorite fuel used, being inexpensive (until recent years), clean and plenty hot. Many 'shiners attach a pump of some sort to their fuel tank—even a bicycle pump—to put pressure onto the fuel going to the burners under the still. Usually, the burners consist of pipes with tiny holes bored in them. Under pressure, the flames give off a tremendous roar. "I've heard the roar a quarter mile up a holler," an ex-agent recalled.

Chapter 8

Revenooers

Duff Floyd (federal revenooer) caught me twice. He just out-run me one time over at Carter's Quarter. I had on a pair of rubber hip boots and had 75 dollars in silver in my pocket. Quarters, nickels, dimes. Duff absolutely out-run me. I could have got away if I'd had on a pair of shoes and hadn't had that 75 dollars in silver.

— *Taft Densmore*
Dawson County, Ga.

Revenooers

THE BIG LAW AND THE LITTLE LAW

Moonshiners across northeast Georgia mourned in 1960 when they heard that the late Bub Kay, a federal revenuer for 35 years, had been killed in an automobile crash. Old timers remembered how he would creep up on the mountain moonshine stills at early dawn, call out the moonshiners by name (which meant there was no need to run), then accompany them home for breakfast. "No use missing a good meal for the kind they serve in jails," he would declare. Kay liked to recount the time he had a still under surveillance at Persimmon, Georgia, as the young makers were admiring the fruits of their craftsmanship. "Yes, sir, this is a good run," one of the makers allowed. "Wish old Bub was around to see it. I believe I'll just call him up." The moonshiner grabbed a pine sapling, twisted a branch like an old telephone crank. "Hello Bub," the boy yelled into his phone. "Hello yourself, son," Bub said, as he stepped from behind a big poplar tree.

In photo above, Bub Kay prepared to dismantle a steamer distillery boiler in Rabun County, Ga.

When David Ayers started out as a lawman in the 1920s in Franklin County, Georgia, the little community of Gum Log, on the border next to South Carolina, had a notorious reputation as a producer of white whiskey. "When I started out as a deputy sheriff, we'd catch as high as five liquor cars a night. All loaded, most with 90 to 120 gallons of liquor apiece, headed to Asheville, North Carolina and Anderson and Greenville, South Carolina. One morning in 1929, the sheriff and I were in our car beside the road, hid. Had a big old Studebaker. This car, loaded with 120 gallons of liquor, came up the road. We could see it coming, early in the morning, way around the curve on a hill over there, coming out of Gum Log. We pulled down in between these big banks. It was a narrow road, and we sorta crossed the car in the road. The trippers couldn't go on either side. They had a big old Chrylser Coupe. Boy from Asheville, North Carolina. Hit us 30 miles an hour or more. He thought the sheriff would move out of the way. Liked to killed the tripper. What hurt him, when he hit the sheriff's car, those cases of liquor stacked up in the back pushed him up against the steering wheel. Cracked some ribs."

Homer Powell, former ATF agent who worked "Tobacco Road" along with the other moonshine-producing areas around Augusta, Georgia, between 1956 and 1961, always wore dark green clothing in order to blend into the countryside. "And I always carred a spool of black thread and a can of dog food with me," he said. "Moonshiners would tie black thread in a perimeter of two hundred yeards around their still about knee high. When they came back to work, if the thread was broken, they'd know the law was close around. I kept the thread to tie it back if I broke it. I kept the dog food to get the moonshiners' dogs on my side." Powell learned a lot of the moonshiners' tricks when he worked against them as an ATF Agent. "They would drop a coin or a knife on the ground close to their still site. If you picked it up, you just bought yourself a dead still. They'd be on to you." Powell also said, "One thing an officer has *got* to do when he visits a still site where the mash is fermenting is to taste the mash to tell when it's going to be ready for running. If you taste it and it's relatively tasteless, it's a few days away from being ready. The first day, the mash is clear on top. After the first day, it forms a thick cap, up to three inches, on the surface. Looks like sawdust, depending on the type grain used, whether it's corn meal or chicken feed. The poorer moonshiners use chicken feed. The cap gets thinner and thinner before the run. When it's ready to run, the cap disappears and the mash is very sour."

Frank Rickman's father, the late Luther Rickman, was sheriff of Rabun County, Georgia for more than 24 years. Said Frank, "I used to go on still raids, from the time the Revenue took turns carrying me on their back. I got to be a pretty good 'catch-dog'. I could run good in rough territory. It made you feel sorta funny, though, going to school in the morning when you had caught your best buddy's daddy at the stillhouse the day before, and I was only 14 or 15. The way we done it, whoever was the catch dog would always go around and get on the hill above the still and then Daddy, he knew everybody bettern' anybody, he'd always come up the cove to the still. Naturally, they would run the opposite way from the still. By us gettin' up there, by the time they (moonshiners) ran up to where we were, they would be run down. All we had to do was get out there and catch 'em."

Photo made at Clayton, Ga., in front of the Rabun County Courthouse about 1938. Sheriff Luther Rickman at left shows off one of his seizures, a giant whiskey still from the Persimmon Valley area, an early type of "hog" still, in which the makers worked off their mash and distilled it in the same pot. In the background is 15-year-old Frank Rickman, even then a muscular "catch dog" on moonshine still raids. At right is Harley McCall, deputy sheriff. As Frank Rickman recalled it, the role of the moonshine informer was a precarious one and he was often hated with much more animosity than that directed toward the lawmen. There was the time when Sheriff Rickman was directed by an informer—a "reporter"—toward an active still. As they walked down a trail toward the still, they came face to face with the three men who were running the still, coming right down from it. The sheriff whirled around—did an about face—and snapped the handcuffs on the reporter and turned back around to the three and asked them what they were doing there.

"We're bee-huntin', Sheriff," they said.

"There's too much of this bee-huntin' a-going on around here. I believe there's a still right around here. I got a feller right here (pointing to the man in handcuffs) that's a bee-huntin'."

At that point, the sheriff took the handcuffs off of the informer and turned him loose to go on back down the trail with the rest.

"If he hadn't a-popped those handcuffs on him," Frank said, "they might have killed him later."

The revenue agents played on the natural competition between moonshiners. When they would catch one, they'd tell him, "We're not going to tell you who reported you, but he lives close." Usually, the arrested violator would say, "We know who he is" and then they'd usually tell on him.

"The Revenue people got these moonshiners to tellin' on each other," Frank Rickman said, "They got more information from the moonshiners themselves than from people on the outside."

"SHORT" STANTON (L) of Greene County, Tennessee, with retired Federal Revenue man, Colonel L. B. Britton, who captured him one time on a still raid. They became the best of friends, a relationship that is not at all unique among former adversaries in the illicit whiskey enterprise. Said Stanton: "I never did make any mean likker. Ask any man in Greene County, North Caroliny, or wherever they drunk any of my likker. It was always good. And you got to keep your distillery clean, particularly those fittins. I forget now which one of these Revenue officers told it right here in federal court. Said they could eat right off the top of the furnace of my still, it was so clean. After a run, you got to take good scalding water and a big rag and wash them barrels and when that cap stays around there, you've got to wash that off perfectly clean, if you make good likker. If you don't, you leave that thar, you'll have old funk likker. It don't taste right, tastes right funky." Short Stanton died sometime after the above photo was made.

Retired Federal Agent Duff Floyd of Jasper, now retired and aged 80, takes it easy with his wife Marjorie on his front porch at Jasper, Georgia. For 35 years, Floyd was one of the major still busters in the Appalachians.

Appalachian Ex-Moonshiners & Revenuers Convention, Dahlonega, Ga.
L-R: TV cameraman, Ex-moonshiner Theodore King, Bill Hardman, then
owner of Gold Hills of Dahlonega, David Ayers, retired state revenue agent,
of Cornelia. Ayers caught King in a mock raid for TV cameras.

Pride in craftsmanship was obvious here as a resident of a deep southwest Georgia county—just arrested at his tiny still—agreed to pose with the state, federal and county officers who had just caught him. On first glance, it would appear this was an upright copper pot still. Actually, it's a drum distillery and the boiler, or pot, is the drum on the left, and the condenser was inside the vertical container at right.

Jesse James Bailey of Asheville, N.C., was one of the greatest still busters in the Appalachians. He was sheriff of Madison County, N.C., on the Tennessee border (known as "Bloody Madison," and later was sheriff of Buncombe County, N.C.

Once there was a time when a feller with an ounce of guts in his hide could have a business of his own.

=/=

Mr Joe Dabney,—

I read your article to the Editor of my
home town paper asking readers afout making corn
liquor (moonshine). I take it that you must be a
rather ~~man~~ young man living in a big city and so
never had a chance to know nothing about making
moonshine liquor. You say you want funny accounts
or tall tales afout this here moonshineing, there
aint much fun in it cause here in the Mountains
of Southwest Va. its a serious and dangerous
business that still goes on but not so much as before.

Have you all read the books that John Fox wrote,
if you havent you should and thus get a good idea
about Mountaineers and how we have to feud an
fight, or at least we did years ago. I am an old
man now but I have seen and ~~experienced~~ much
in my younger days. I have witnessed gun
fights and know of ~~other~~ many cases of fatal fights
that was brought on because of moonshine ing.

As a young man I lived near a big mountain

and hunted in this mountain for many, many years
and many times I have seen moonshine stills in
operation, but the law of the mountaineer was to tell
nothing, and see nothing wrong against any one. If
you talked to much, or told the County law about a
moonshine still you could'nt expect to live long.

The code of the mountain men was simple but
strict. I never fooled with moonshineing or boot-
legging, I was a farmer and was trusted and well
liked by all, both out law and law abiding.

Only once was I came near to being shot up by
moonshiners when I came near their still while
squirrel hunting, they chased me a mile and fired
many shots at me. I never did know who they
were, must of been strangers, maybe thought I
was revoorner or law man. While out hunting
rabbits I found five gallons moonshine liquor in a little
washout gulley. I let it alone. I saw eight quarts hid
in a hollow tree stump. I found 8 gallons in a small
cave. I darn sure did'nt bother any of it ever. Over
the years back then I have seen much moonshine
whiskey hidden in various places.

=3=

I reckon I haven't drunk any moonshine whiskey for nigh on to thirty years now. Back in younger years there was good peach brandy, Apple brandy, Corn whiskey, Cherry wine, Blackberry wine, Grape wine etc. That there Corn whiskey was called white lighting, stagger & fall, head bust, rot gut, white mule and Tommy hawk, it sure was powerful and sometimes it contained toffacco juice, a little bit of Lye, maybe colored with a little iodine or Oak tree bark. Some was real good, some real bad. Its still being made today back in the mountains but I advise for no man to drink it now. I reckon I am sorry for you young men of today, crowded up in big cities, no freedom as I have had all my life in the hills, valleys and mountains. A man was a man then, or else he didn't last long. A dollar was big money then, I have worked for 15¢ a day, cutting timber, hauling logs, plowing cornfields, cutting wheat, hay, or corn etc. Anything to make a dollar honest.

Its a pity you young people of today can't have some of the good living like I have had about 75 or 80 years ago.   No name — Just Old Mountain Man.

Gallery
of
Pictures

Hubert Howell, now re-
tired in Cartersville, Ga.,
moonshined in Cherokee
County, Ga. during the depression years.

Maud Thacker
checks
out her wine
makings.

203

This cabin (above) was occupied by Thomas Jefferson ("Tom Jeff") Cupp until his death several years ago.

Very rare now, this type of moonshine still is generally known as a "solid copper turnip bottom" outfit.

The late Thomas Jefferson Cupp, "Tom Jeff" to his friends, was the patriarch among the corn whiskey clan in the Cumberland Gap range of southwest Virginia.

Retired Federal Agent Duff Floyd (R) and retired Georgia State Revenue Agent David Ayers (second from left) enjoyed meeting up with their old associates and adversaries at the Appalachian Ex-Moonshiners and Revenuers convention in Dahlonega, Ga.